The Best of Collectible Dinnerware

Jo Cunningham

Schiffer Publishing Ltd

77 Lower Valley Road, Atglen, PA 19310

Dedication

This book is dedicated to the true master potter, God's indescribable gift-His son, Jesus. He is the potter who is reshaping my life, molding me and making me in his likeness. The potter to whom I have surrendered my life and, in return, He has given me forgiveness and eternal life. Jesus truly is King of Kings and Lord of Lords and the greatest potter of them all.

Copyright © 1995 by Jo Cunningham.

Printed in China.
ISBN: 0-88740-833-8

Cunningham, Jo.
    The best of collectible dinnerware: with values/Jo Cunningham.
        p.   cm – (A Schiffer book for collectors)
    Includes bibliographical references and index.
    ISBN 0-88740-833-8
    1. Ceramic tableware–Collectors and collecting–United States.
    2. Pottery–20th century–Collectors and collecting–United States.
    I. Title. II. Series.
    NK4695.T33C84   1995
    738.3'0973'075–dc20   95-8474
                                                      CIP

Published by Schiffer Publishing, Ltd.
77 Lower Valley Road
Atglen, PA 19310
Please write for a free catalog.
This book may be purchased from the publisher.
Please include $2.95 postage.
Try your bookstore first.

We are interested in hearing from authors
with book ideas on related subjects.

The Best of

Acknowledgments

It is a difficult task to sufficiently thank and properly acknowledge all of those who have helped with this project. So many friends have shared so much, either in deeds or by encouraging words.

With that said, I will try, in some way, to convey my thanks and appreciation beginning with my family. As families go, they have endured the most and have always supported my many projects. Everyone has tolerated stacks of trade publications, magazines and catalogs much longer than they should have. My husband, Wayne, has been the driver on trips, the packer at the photography sessions and all-round helper.

This project could never have progressed without the support of my daughter, Terry Graves. She has typed the copy, rewritten and written copy, coped with three children and a new computer and has somehow maintained her sanity. A very special thanks for all the help she has always given me. We're a team!

Most of the pieces shown in *The Best of Collectible Dinnerware* are from the collection of Bill Stratton. Everyone should have a dish-buddy, one who speaks dish-talk, shares his or her finds, information, and is willing to loan dishes for a project such as this.

Photography was done by Leland and Crystal Payton. The Paytons are authors of books on collectibles and understand what is necessary to get just the right shot. Mr. Leland and his assistant, Miss Crystal, made the photography sessions a lot of fun. I went into this photographic arrangement knowing the Paytons casually. I now consider them my friends. Thank you both for your help.

This project was enhanced by information received from librarians from several different parts of the country. For all of those who contributed information, loaned pieces to be photographed, sent pictures, or supported this book with your encouraging words, a very special and sincere thank you.

Special thanks to:

Charles Alexander, Everett Allen, Betty Goodan Andrews, Rich Barilla, LaRaye Bess, Tom & Phyllis Bess, Bert J. Brock, Patsy Button, Gary Buzbee, Ed Carson, Michael Cochran, Jenny Derwich, Nicki Duncan, Delleen Enge, Barbara Erwin, Emerson Fraunfelter, Carl Gibbs, Susan Gibson, Jerri Graves, Richard and Linda Guffey, Doris and Burdell Hall, Ben Hughes, Ann Kerr, Allen Kleinbeck, Terry Kramer, Carrie Loretz, Johnnie and Bonnie McCroskey, Jackie Bess-Minnick, Naomi's of San Francisco, Harriett Neely, Leland and Crystal Payton, Paul H. Preo, Beverly Reed, Jim Reed, Irving Richards, Jean Riddle, Jim Riebel, Carol Sandler, Marvin Spragg, Mary Jo Stanton, Billy Stratton, Don Schreckengost, Viktor Schreckengost, Robert Vossler, Joel Wilson, Eva Zeisel, and Sibylle Zemitis.

Special thanks also to:

Brand Library and Art Galleries, Glendale, California, California State Library, Sacramento, California, Kansas City Public Library, Kansas City, Missouri, Pikes Peak Library District, Colorado Springs, Colorado, Riverside City and County Public Library, Riverside, California, Rochester Public Library, Rochester, New York, San Antonio Area Library System, San Antonio, Texas, Springfield Art Museum Library, Springfield, Missouri, Springfield Public Library Reference Staff, Springfield, Missouri, Strong Museum Library, Rochester, New York, and Texas State Library, Austin, Texas

Introduction

The Best of Collectible Dinnerware is the fulfillment of my dream to present to collectors the best and most currently collected dinnerware of American and other pottery and china companies. In Ecclesiastes, chapter 5, verse 3(a), we are told "For a dream comes with much business and painful effort" and this dream has certainly been no exception to that scripture.

It has been my intention to provide a guide of the most collected dinnerware. I realize that you may collect a pattern that is not included in this book. This in no way diminishes the importance of your collection, nor have we attempted to show or list all pieces in all the patterns shown.

Information, various pieces and pricing have all graciously been provided by collectors. Prices may be higher or lower in your particular area. Please do let us know about price varia-

tions in your area and availability of the items shown in *The Best of Collectible Dinnerware*. Your input would be invaluable in further developing helpful price guides for the future.

The Best of Collectible Dinnerware is arranged differently than most alphabetical arrangements. This book is divided into sections and then broken down alphabetically. Most of the names used in *The Best of Collectible Dinnerware* are official names. In some instances, the correct name was not available to me and I gave it a name. When this occurs, the name I gave to the item appears in quotes.

You are invited to write me at 535 E. Normal, Springfield, Missouri 65807. If you require a reply, please include a self-addressed stamped envelope. Not only will a SASE be appreciated, it will facilitate a speedy reply.

Chapter One: The Best of Blue and White

Buffalo Pottery backstamp.

Blue Willow

The blue on white decorations have been popular with collectors for many years. One of the oldest and longest running patterns sought after by collectors is Blue Willow.

According to Minnie Kamm in her book *Old Dishes*, Blue Willow dates back to 1772. Blue Willow has been produced by many companies with even more variations. One of the most popular American made Blue Willow patterns was produced by the Buffalo China Company, Buffalo, New York.

Row 1: Blue Willow cup and saucer, dinner plate, dinner plate (with design variation). Row 2: Utility pitcher, sugar, creamer, covered pitcher.

Row 1: Blue Willow Covered vegetable, covered cheese or butter dish.

Liberty Blue

Liberty Blue was a 1976 grocery store premium item. The blue on white Staffordshire ironstone depicts different Historic Colonial Scenes. Liberty Blue was made in England and is becoming quite collectible. Prices for Liberty Blue are rising rapidly. The impressive platter is bringing $100 on the collector's market.

Liberty Blue 1977 full page advertisement. *Reprinted with permission of Ramey's Supermarkets, Springfield, Missouri.*

Liberty Blue sugar, creamer, large platter, teapot.

Row 1: Liberty Blue gravy boat, platter, dessert plate, dinner plate. Row 2: Platter, small platter or liner, cup/saucer set, covered quarter pound butter.

Provincial Blue

Provincial Blue by Metlox is a very popular pattern with collectors. The large platter is a very unusual and hard to find piece of Provincial Blue.

Row 1: Metlox Provincial Blue large serving platter, flour canister with wooden lid. Row 2: Platter, gravy boat, covered vegetable, small plate, small plate and bowl, covered sugar, cup and saucer, ashtray.

Liberty Blue backstamp.

Chapter Two: The Best of The Big Five of California

The fine qualities of the California clays were discovered soon after the Spanish padres established their missions along the California coast, but the California potteries that collectors know best had their beginnings in 1909 when the Bauer family moved their pottery from Kentucky. Natural clay and allied materials were found in abundance in California. The process of adding talc, later called the Malinite process, improved the quality of California ware.

By the late 1930s, Bauer; Gladding, McBean & Co.; Metlox; Pacific Clay Products; and Vernon Kilns were referred to as "The Big California Five" in their advertising at that time.

By 1949, it was reported that nearly half the tableware made in the United States was being produced in California. In the 1950s, small California potteries were no longer able to compete with foreign imports and plastics and many of them closed their doors.

I must confess that as many dishes as I have handled, the wares from Metlox; Vernon; and Gladding, McBean & Co., continued to confuse me. To help myself out of this confusion, I made a diagram of the "Big Five." It proved to be helpful to me so I include it here for your use. (See page 11)

The California section begins with the "Big Five" and some of their wares and then continues to cover other California potteries such as Brock, Flintridge, Santa Anita, Wallace, and Weil.

CALIFORNIA POTTERY GUILD

526 Chamber of Commerce Bldg.
LOS ANGELES

California Pottery Guild advertisement featuring items from "The Big Five."
Reprinted from *Creative Design*, 1937.

The Big California Five

Bauer family moves from Kentucky

1909   Establish Bauer Pottery

Had pottery in Kentucky prior to moving to California.

1875   Founded as a sewer pipe manufacturing company by Charles Gladding, George Chambers & Peter McBean

1923   Purchased Tropico

1933   Purchased Am. Encaustic Tiling

1937   Bought Catalina Island Pottery

1962   Merged to form Intnl. Pipe & Ceramics

1963   Changed name to Interpace

1974   Sold Franciscan Div. to Wedgwood

1927   Founded by W. Prouty – ceramic part of neon signs

1947   Sold to Evan K. Shaw – Reorganized

1958   Bought patterns & goodwill from Vernon Kilns

1958   Ceased using name Vernon Kilns

1958   Organized Vernonware division of Metlox

1932   Founded as a sewer pipe manufacturer

1916   Founded by George Poxon as Poxon China

1928   Became Vernon Potteries

1931   Purchased by F. G. Bennison

1931   Name changed to Vernon Kilns

1958   Sold trade names and goodwill to Metlox

Bauer Pottery
Los Angeles, CA

1927   Bauer produced colored kitchenware

1932   Added colored bright dinnerware

1940's   Bauer marked Bockman Pottery

1950-51   Herb Brushé produced Contempo and El Fresco at Bauer

Gladding McBean Mfg. Co.
LA and Glendale

Early part of manufacturing was terra cotta and sewer tiles

1934   Introduced Franciscan Ware El Patio

1942   Added Franciscan Fine China

1984   Closed

Metlox
Manhattan Beach

1927   Produced tableware

Prouty lowered production cost by inventing several machines that increased production

1934   Poppy Trail was produced

1959   Poppytrail became one word

Pacific Clay Products
Los Angeles

1932   Began producing bright colored dinnerware

Late 30's added pastel colors

Discontinued pottery lines war years

Never went back to pottery manufacturing

Vernon Kilns
Los Angeles

Early 1930's solid colorware marked Bird Pottery

Late 1930's produced solid color lines each one called 'something' California. Early California
     Late California
     Ultra California
     Native California

Produced many other successful patterns

Bauer

J.A. Bauer established his Los Angeles plant about 1909, moving his pottery business from Kentucky. In its earlier years, the pottery's main business was making and selling flower pots, stoneware and miscellaneous outdoor items--garden and patio ware.

The Bauer Company began to use color in their kitchenware line about 1927. They were one of the first potteries to produce brightly colored solid glazed dinnerware. Their Ring design was introduced about 1934.

Collectors of Bauer Pottery may find some pieces marked "Bockman Quality Pottery." This mark can be found on their wartime crockery that was made specifically for producers of food. When Bauer was experiencing labor difficulties, Red Wing Pottery supplied ware for them. Herb Brusche, husband of Mr. Bauer's granddaughter, became part of the Bauer operation in the early 1950s. He brought out a line called Contempo and another called Al Fresco. These lines were marked with the Brusche mark.

Country Gardens are experimental pieces made by Bauer for Mary Wright, the wife of Russel Wright. She was an artist and designer in her own right. Limited amounts of ware designed by her were sold. Consider it rare when and if you find Mary Wright's Country Gardens.

Bauer closed its doors in the late 1950s as did many other California potteries.

Row 1: Bauer Ring jar, large mixing bowl. Row 2: Ring small bowl, refrigerator stack set, creamer, utility pitcher.

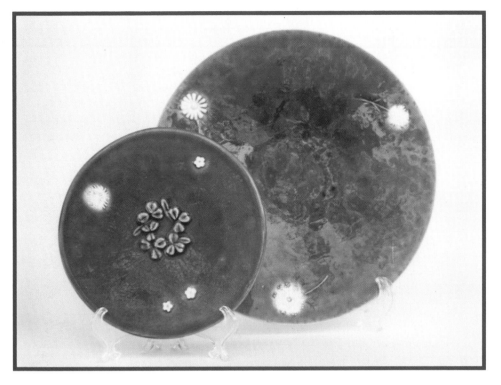

Decorated Country Gardens Both experimental pieces for Bauer by Mary Wright.

Country Gardens.

Gladding, McBean & Co.

Gladding, McBean & Co. was organized in 1875 as a sewer pipe and tile manufacturer. The company did not begin producing dinnerware until 1934 when they introduced their first colored dinnerware--El Patio.

The discovery of adding talc (magnesium silicate) to clay was an important breakthrough for the pottery industry in California. Gladding, McBean & Co. was able to purchase this formula from Willis Prouty, son of the formula's originator, T.C. Prouty. Dr. Malinowsky, the ceramic engineer at Gladding, McBean & Co., improved the formula, allowing them to make a stronger body that could be fired at lower temperatures. This improvement became known as the Malinite process. They were also the first pottery to develop a true Chinese red from silenium.

Gladding, McBean & Co. added a line of fine china in 1942. Both earthenware and china were marketed under the Franciscan name under the direction of Frederick Grant II, former president of Weller Pottery Company.

1970s Franciscan Kaleidoscope.

Franciscan Tiempo. Reprinted from *China, Glass and Decorative Accessories*, October 1949.

OLD CALIFORNIA
IN NEW *Catalina Pottery*

RANCHO Dinnerware with its rare simplicity of line and harmony of typical CATALINA colors is a perfect type of informal service — truly expressive of old Californian hospitality.

•

Many pieces of unusual design make the CATALINA art pottery lines exceptionally interesting.

Catalina Pottery

GLADDING. McBEAN & CO., LOS ANGELES, CALIFORNIA

Late 1930s Gladding, McBean & Co. Catalina Pottery.

★ INSIDE A COLOR....

OUTSIDE... SATIN IVORY

It is
THE NEW...THE SMART
Duotone

...emphasizing the trend to elegance in colored tableware.

Our exquisite satin ivory is used outside and each piece is lined with a delicate color of matchless beauty...coral, blue, yellow or green.

A service for four...complete with serving pieces...will be the outstanding feature of fashion-alert china departments this Fall.

Catalina Pottery

Send for descriptive folder in r and name of nearest dealer

ADDING, McBEAN & CO. • LOS ANGELES, CALIFORNIA

QUALITY COUNTS
with
Rancho Ware
REG. U. S. PAT. OFF.

Glowing are the colors and delightfully simple the shapes of RANCHO WARE ...and very important is the exceptionally tough and durable body that will not leak or craze...for charming informal table settings.

Catalina Pottery

A folder showing shapes and colors sent on request
GLADDING, McBEAN & CO., LOS ANGELES

Late 1930s advertisement showing Gladding, McBean & Co. Catalina line-Rancho Ware.

Late 1930s advertisement showing Gladding, McBean & Co. Catalina line-Duotone.

This Color Counts!

IMPERIAL MING YELLOW—a yellow with unbelievable depth of quality and vibrancy. • FRANCISCAN'S DEL ORO Dinnerware presents Imperial Ming Yellow in a delightfully fresh treatment of color-and-white handled with modern simplicity. • DEL ORO is made in a full dinnerware line and is available for immediate delivery.

FRANCISCAN WARE

Reg. U. S. Pat. Off.

GLADDING McBEAN & CO., LOS ANGELES, CALIFORNIA • NEW YORK OFFICE: JUSTIN THARAUD, INC., 129 FIFTH AVE.

Gladding, McBean & Co. Franciscan Ware-Del Oro pattern.

Row 1: Gladding, McBean & Co. Red Apple mug, creamer, large platter, teapot. Row 2: Snack tray with tumbler, tumbler, quarter pound butter.

Row 1: Gladding, McBean & Co. Red Apple sherbet/dessert, mixing bowl, plate, syrup pitcher, egg cup, candle holder. Row 2: Gravy boat and liner, salt and pepper shakers, soup bowl, ashtray, mug, covered soup, teacup and saucer, glass tumbler.

FRANCISCAN
Desert Rose

You can have flowers on your table

every day when DESERT ROSE blooms

on your dinnerware. This hand-painted design

is color-locked under a brilliant glaze

that keeps it ever bright-as-new.

Oven-safe—sturdily resistant to breakage.

Franciscan Ware by Gladding, McBean & Co., Los Angeles, Calif.

Left:
Desert Rose is another favorite of collectors in Gladding, McBean's hand painted lines. Introduced a year after Apple, Desert Rose is said to be one of the most successful dinnerware patterns ever produced.

Opposite Page:
Franciscan Poppy was introduced in 1950. Poppy was reported to be a hit at the 1950 summer trade shows. Poppy was introduced on a new coupe shape. Franciscan Poppy is in shorter supply than Apple and Desert Rose as it did not have the long run of the other two patterns.

New Pattern...New Coupe Shape...

New FRANCISCAN POPPY

Tops at the Summer Shows

PRE-TESTED FOR APPEAL, Franciscan Poppy is the latest, sale-sparking pattern in famed Franciscan Ware. Embossed and hand-decorated on a new and modern coupe shape, Franciscan Poppy catches the eye with its warm, bright colors...gay as the wild flowers that carpet the sunswept fields of California ...and — because it's Franciscan — *it will never craze.* It appears this month in a hard-selling, full-color ad in the Ladies' Home Journal where its sparkling beauty will attract millions of potential customers.

IDEAL FOR DISPLAY—in windows and showcases, on counters and shelves — Franciscan Poppy will push your volume and profits to new, year-end highs.

TIE IN FOR PROFITS with the national promotion of the new Starter-ette* (eight piece service for two) on most of Franciscan's popular patterns.   *TRADEMARK

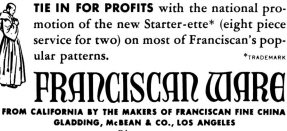

FRANCISCAN WARE

FROM CALIFORNIA BY THE MAKERS OF FRANCISCAN FINE CHINA
GLADDING, McBEAN & CO., LOS ANGELES
Since 1875

Row 1: Franciscan Starburst plate, platter, cup and saucer. Row 2: Vegetable bowl, ashtray, quarter pound butter dish, dessert plate, small bowl.

Row 1: Franciscan Autumn platter, salt and pepper, pitcher. Row 2: Vinegar and oil cruet, creamer and sugar, ashtray, dessert plate, tidbit servers.

Row 1: Franciscan china Lorraine (maroon) dinner plate, platter, cream soup and liner. Row 2: Cup and saucer, creamer and sugar, vegetable bowl.

Franciscan backstamp for Lorraine china.

Metlox Manufacturing Company, Inc.

The beginning of Metlox Manufacturing Company dates back to 1927 when Willis and T.C. Prouty became interested in producing the ceramic portion of neon signs. Metlox Manufacturing Company was incorporated in the state of California in 1933. The president of Metlox Manufacturing Company, Inc., was Willis Prouty, son of T.C. Prouty.

Willis Prouty was responsible for Metlox's Poppy Trail line that was introduced in 1934. He is also credited with patenting several machines that increased the speed and lowered costs of production.

Metlox did not contribute much of importance in the way of dinnerware until 1947 when Evan K. Shaw and Robert L. Peaslee purchased controlling interest and reorganized the company. They were very concerned with "originality in design" and introduced the California Ivy pattern. In 1959, the Poppytrail mark became one word.

Metlox Manufacturing Company's incorporation was terminated on January 4, 1988.

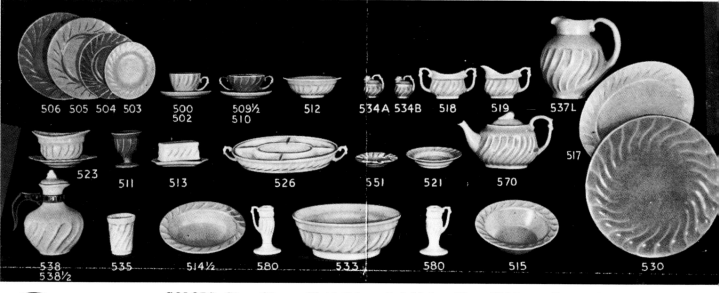

COLORS: Gloss Glazes, Vivid Colors: Delphinium Blue, Old Rose, Canary Yellow, Turquoise Blue, Poppy Orange and Rust.

Satin Glazes, Pastel Colors: Opaline Green, Powder Blue, Petal Pink, Pastel Yellow, Satin Turquoise, Peach and Satin Ivory.

Early Metlox Yorkshire brochure.

● *Pintoria* COLORS: Gloss Glazes, Vivid Colors: Delphinium Blue, Old Rose, Canary Yellow, Turquoise Blue, Poppy Orange and Rust.

DINNERWARE ☆ BEVERAGEWARE ☆ KITCHENWARE

Metlox brochure showing Pintoria and Poppytrail.

California Ivy pitcher. Metlox's prolific output of superior designs was credited to Bob Shaw and Mel Allen, art directors for the Metlox China Company.

Metlox California Ivy from 1950 brochure.

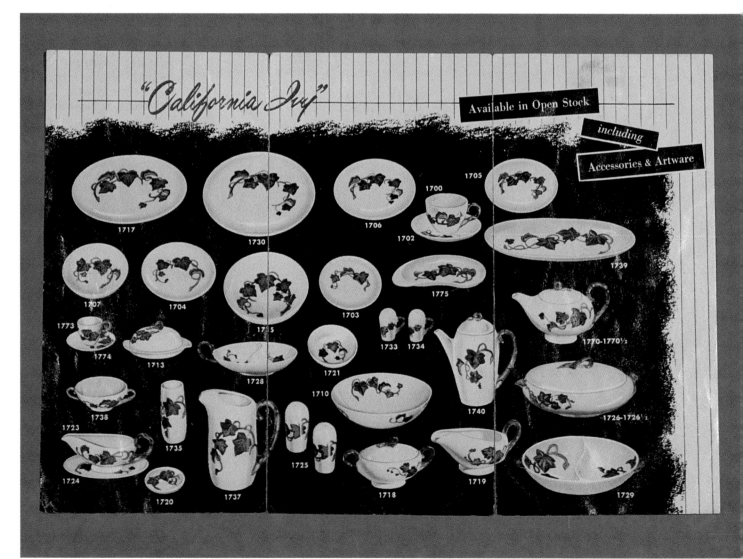

Metlox California Ivy from 1950 brochure.

Row 1: Metlox Jamestown Provincial gravy boat with wooden handle, coffee server with wooden knob, dinner plate, bowl with handle. Row 2: Sugar with wooden handle, salt and pepper, sugar bowl, vinegar and oil cruet, cup and saucer, bread tray.

Row 1: Metlox Provincial Blue pepper mill, teapot, utility pitcher, Cape Cod creamer and sugar. Row 2: Metlox Provincial Blue bowl, creamer, divided bowl, Cape Cod quarter pound butter dish.

JAMESTOWN
PROVINCIAL

Poppytrail -METLOX

Safe in oven and
dishwasher • Durable
Made in Calif. • U.S.A.

Poppytrail

POTTERY

POPPYTRAIL
BY
METLOX
MADE IN CALIFORNIA

Metlox Camellia pattern.

Metlox Antique Grape plate, cup and saucer.

Row 1: Metlox Vernon Tulip cup and saucer, dinner plate, sugar and creamer. Row 2: Cereal bowl, salt and pepper, dessert plate, bowl.

Row 1: Metlox Floralace creamer, gravy boat and liner, covered sugar.
Row 2: Cup and saucer, salt and pepper.

Row 1: Metlox Vernon Ware Vineyard dinner plate, platter, sugar and creamer. Row 2: Dessert plate, cup and saucer, vegetable bowl, small bowl, salt and pepper, gravy boat and liner.

Metlox Potteries

With several main scenes set at the dinner table, the dinnerware in the new movie "Shenandoah" is said to be getting a real publicity break from its exposure in the film. The pattern is "Vineyard," by the Vernonware Division of Metlox Potteries.

forty-one

Vernon Ware Vineyard backstamp.

Cast from the movie *Shenandoah* shown sitting at a table set with Metlox Vernon Ware Vineyard dinnerware. *China, Glass & Tableware*, October 1965. *Reprinted with permission of Doctorow Communications, Inc., Clifton, N.J.*

Metlox California Strawberry cup and saucer, dinner plate, dessert plate, bowl.

Metlox California Strawberry backstamp.

Metlox "Rooster" creamer, sugar, dinner plate, salt and pepper, dessert plate.

Row 1: Metlox Red Rooster pitcher, platter, coffee server. Row 2: Salt and pepper, coffee mug, cup and saucer, sugar and creamer.

Metlox California Provincial three-tiered serving tray.

Metlox Homestead creamer, sugar, plate, mug.

Row 1: Metlox "Rose" platter, platter, dessert plate. Row 2: Divided bowl,
salt and pepper, quarter pound butter dish, sugar and creamer.

Pacific Clay Products

Very little is known about Pacific Clay Products (also called Pacific Pottery). We know that it was located in Los Angeles, California. Like many California pottery companies, it started as a manufacturer of sewer pipes and "staple stoneware products" in 1886.

Pacific began production of dinnerware in 1932 with M.J. Lattie in charge of the art department. Pacific's first dinnerware was made up of vivid reds, blues, greens and yellows. These vivid colors were later changed to pastel colors. Coralitos was one of their late 1930s pattern names.

During the Second World War the company made products for the defense effort and never resumed producing dinnerware. In a letter from David Hollingsworth, the president of Pacific Clay Products, he states that none of the facilities used in dinnerware production are currently in use. Pacific Clay Products now makes clay pipe, face brick, firebacks and other structural clay products.

A reprint of a 1934 Pacific Pottery catalogue shows a wide variety of pieces in their Hostess line. Pacific Hostessware was available in four standard colors: Apache Red, Pacific Blue, Lemon Yellow and Jade Green. Sierra White, Royal Blue, and Delphinium Blue were also available.

Pacific cheese plate, snack plate, carafe, divided plate, gravy boat. *Courtesy of Naomi's of San Francisco.*

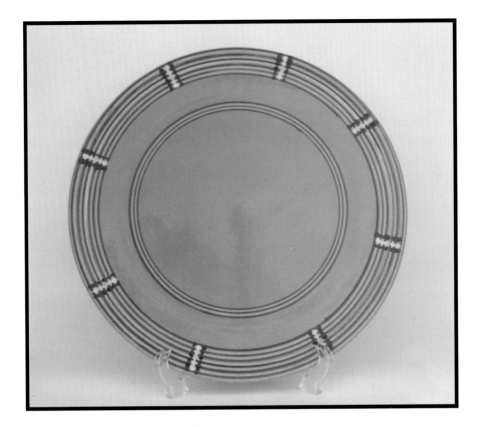

Pacific blue decorated plate.

A DIMITY PATTERN, blue design on yellow body, makes an informal breakfast or luncheon service for four. This comes in sets of 23 pieces which retail around $13.95 a set, including two sizes of plates, coffee cups and saucers, onion soup bowls and saucers, toast platter, sugar bowl and creamer. An ovenware pie-plate with detachable wood handles comes in two sizes—10" (illustrated) and 8". Available in the following plain colors—red, yellow, blue, green, delphinium, turquoise, apricot and white; with a pumpkin design on red or blue; and with apple design on yellow or white. Pacific Clay Products.

Advertisement for Pacific Dimity pattern from 1937 *Creative Design* magazine.

Pacific backstamp.

Decorated Pacific was also available. Some of the patterns shown in a 1935 Pacific catalog were Willow, Dimity, Poppy, Wheat, Wheat Spray, Windmill, Crysanthemum, and Fruits. A seven piece game set with a Duck design was also shown.

I regret that the Pacific Catalog would not reproduce well enough for readers to see the Pacific shapes in Hostessware. The 1935 price list, Pacific item number, item and price per dozen are listed in hopes that it will give you an idea of the vast amount of Hostessware made.

Hostess Ware Pottery
All Prices Per Dozen

No.	Description	Price
1	Mixing Bowl, 16¼" Diam.	45.00
2	Mixing Bowl, 14¼" Diam.	24.00
3	Mixing Bowl, 13½" Diam.	21.60
4	Mixing Bowl, 12⅜" Diam.	16.00
6	Mixing Bowl, 11⅜" Diam.	15.00
9	Mixing Bowl, 10¼" Diam.	9.60
12	Mixing Bowl, 9¼" Diam.	6.60
18	Mixing Bowl, 8⅛" Diam.	5.40
24	Mixing Bowl, 6⅞" Diam.	4.20
30	Mixing Bowl, 6" Diam.	3.60
	Nests of Five Bowls, Nos. 9 to 30, incl.	27.00
200	Casserole & Cover, 7" Diam.	16.50
201	7" Casserole & Tray	6.60
202	Casserole & Cover, 8"	19.80
203	8" Casserole Tray	7.80
205	Baking Dish, 4" Diam.	2.40
205-X	Baking Dish, 4" Diam.	1.50
206	Custard Cup, 3¾" Diam.	1.50
207	Butter Chip, 3" Diam.	1.00
208	Ramekin Set	6.00
210	Deep Casserole & Cover, 5" Diam.	10.80
211	Deep Casserole & Cover, 7¼" Diam.	16.50
212	Pudding Dish, 6½" Diam.	6.00
213	Pudding Dish, 7½" Diam.	7.20
214	Pudding Dish, 8½" Diam.	8.40
225-A	⅛-Gal. Bean Pot, 3½" High	4.20
226-A	¼-Gal. Bean Pot, 5¾" High	6.00
227-A	½-Gal. Bean Pot, 6¼" High	9.00
228-A	1-Gal. Bean Pot, 7" High	15.00
231-A	Individual Bean Pot, 3½" High	3.00
300	Pastry Bowl, 8" Diam.	9.00
301	Waffle Bowl, 9¼" Diam.	16.50
302	Egg Beater Bowl	12.00
305	Pretzel Jar	21.00
306	Condiment Jar, 3¾" Diam.	6.00
310	Salad Bowl, 9" Diam.	15.00
311	Salad Bowl, 11" Diam.	21.00
312	Punch Bowl, 14" Diam.	33.00
313	Punch Bowl Cup	3.60
314	Low Salad Bowl, 13" Diam.	24.00
315	Low Salad Bowl, 8" Diam.	10.80
400	Pitcher, 4" Diam.	4.80
401	Pitcher, 1 quart, 5¼" Diam.	6.00
402	Pitcher, 3 pints, 6¼" Diam.	9.00
403	Sugar Bowl, open	9.90

Hostess Ware Pottery (Continued)

403-A	Sugar Bowl Cover	1.50
404	Cream Pitcher	6.60
407	Sugar Bowl, 3" Diam.	6.00
408	Cream Pitcher, 3" Diam.	6.00
409	Tumbler, 3⅛" Diam.	3.60
410	Water Bottle, 9½" High	18.00
411	Tumbler, 4⅛" High	2.40
412	Tray, 10" Diam.	9.60
413	Tray, 15" Diam.	27.00
414	Cheese & Cracker, 16" Diam.	33.00
416	Cheese & Cracker & Cover	18.00
419	Drinking Mug, 5" High	3.60
420	Ball Pitcher	24.00
422	Square Ice Box Pitcher	15.00
424	Refrigerator Dish, 8½" Diam.	14.40
425	Refrigerator Dish, 5 " Diam.	9.60
426	Refrigerator Dish, 3½" Diam.	7.20
430	Pitcher, 8½" High	18.00
431	Tumbler, 4" High	3.60
432	Coaster, 4" Diam.	1.80
433	Footed Goblet, 12 oz.	6.60
439	Individual Tea Pot	15.00
440	Tea Pot, 8 cup	21.00
502	Mug or Stein, 4½" High	5.40
507	Pitcher, 8½" High	15.00
508	Pitcher, approx. 2 qts.	19.80
600	Pie Plate, 9¾" Diam.	9.60
602	Vegetable Dish, 8" Diam.	15.00
603	Relish Dish, 9" Diam.	15.00
604	Covered Soup Tureen	33.00
607	Coffee Cup	6.00
608	Coffee Cup, 3" High	4.80
609	Coffee Cup Saucer, 6" Diam.	3.60
609-A	Tea Cup Saucer	3.60
610	Service Plate, 7½" Diam.	4.80
611	Service Plate, 9" Diam.	7.20
612	Cake Plate, 16" Diam.	27.00
613	Dinner Plate, 11" Diam.	9.00
614	Bread & Butter Plate, 6" Diam. *72.0*	3.60
615	Grill Plate, 11" Diam.	12.00
617	Medium Platter	24.00
619	Chop Plate	18.00
36-A	Cream Soup, W. Handles, 5¼" Diam.	3.60
36-R	Cream Soup	3.00
620 }		
622 }	Salt & Pepper Shakers, Doz. Pr.	15.00
622	Flat Salad Server, 17" Diam.	36.00
623	Low Coupe Bowl, 17" Diam.	36.00
	Lazy Susan	84.00

Listing of Pacific Hostessware pottery from 1935 Pacific catalog.

Pacific Hostessware pottery from 1935 Pacific catalog.

Hostessware

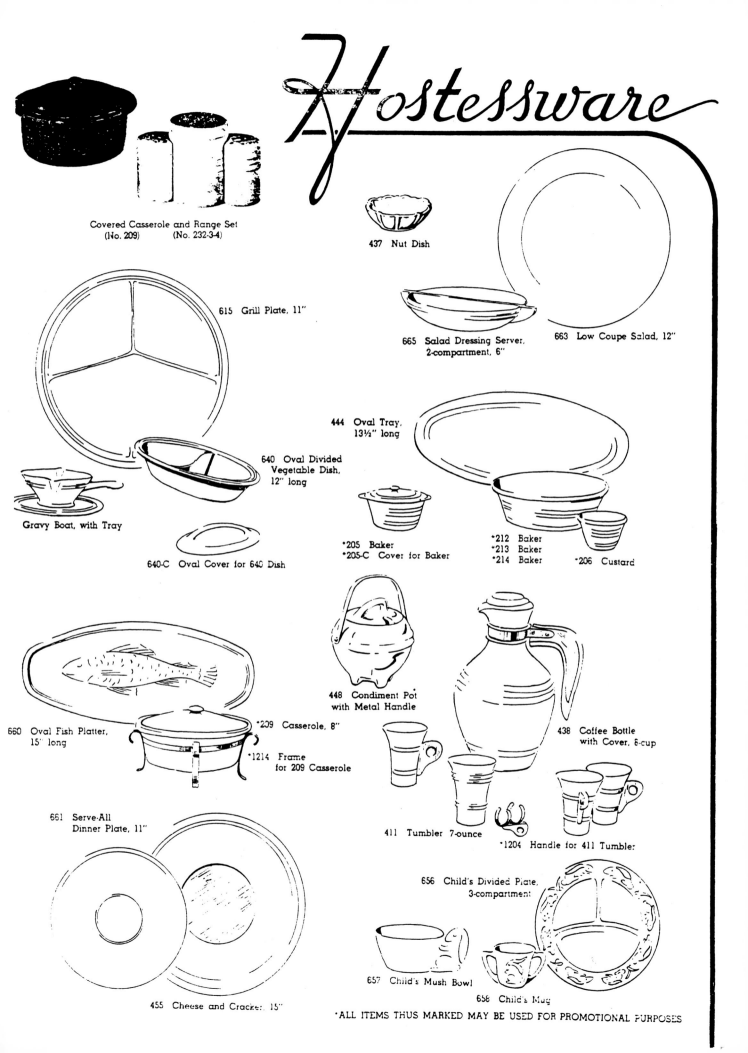

Covered Casserole and Range Set
(No. 209)   (No. 232-3-4)

437 Nut Dish

615 Grill Plate, 11"

665 Salad Dressing Server,
2-compartment, 6"

663 Low Coupe Salad, 12"

444 Oval Tray,
13½" long

640 Oval Divided
Vegetable Dish,
12" long

Gravy Boat, with Tray

640-C Oval Cover for 640 Dish

*205 Baker
*205-C Cover for Baker

*212 Baker
*213 Baker
*214 Baker

*206 Custard

660 Oval Fish Platter,
15" long

448 Condiment Pot
with Metal Handle

438 Coffee Bottle
with Cover, 6-cup

*209 Casserole, 8"

*1214 Frame
for 209 Casserole

411 Tumbler 7-ounce

*1204 Handle for 411 Tumbler

661 Serve-All
Dinner Plate, 11"

656 Child's Divided Plate,
3-compartment

657 Child's Mush Bowl

658 Child's Mug

455 Cheese and Cracker, 15"

*ALL ITEMS THUS MARKED MAY BE USED FOR PROMOTIONAL PURPOSES

Vernon Kilns

Poxon China, predecessor to Vernon Kilns, was founded around 1916 in Vernon, California when George Poxon purchased an existing tile plant. Due to war time government orders for dishes, he later changed the company to a pottery plant that he named Poxon China.

In 1928, George Poxon put his wife in charge of the plant and went on to other ventures. The Poxon China Company then became Vernon Potteries, LTD. In 1931, Vernon Potteries, LTD., was sold to Mr. Faye G. Bennison. At this time, the name of the company became Vernon Kilns, beginning the era of collectible Vernon Kilns ware.

The Metlox Manufacturing Company bought the Vernon Kilns' trade names in 1958. The name of Vernon Kilns ware then became Vernon Ware, later renamed Vernonware.

Vernon Pottery from September 1949 *China, Glass & Decorative Accessories.*

The original Vernon pottery at left with the old-style beehive kiln was built in 1916, a date which farther back than many peop realize. This factory was destroye by the earthquake. Below is ti new Vernon plant, one of the m modern in the world, built after t devastating fire of 1947.

1948 Vernon plate given away as memento of visit to Vernon Kilns Pottery.

Vernon Bird Pottery (pattern name unknown) soup bowl, dinner plate, cup.

Vernon Bird Pottery backstamp.

Vernonware advertisement showing Vernon's Modern California.

"EARLY CALIFORNIA" (right). Brilliant glaze ware in orange, turquoise, green, brown, blue, yellow. Gift Package $5.00, $8.95, $13.95.

"MODERN CALIFORNIA" (above). Delicate pastel ware in pistachio, orchid, straw, azure. Gift Package $5.95, $9.50, $14.95.

ROCKWELL KENT is the designer of these two striking patterns. "MOBY DICK" (above), in walnut brown, dark blue, maroon, light orange. Gift Package $8.95, $15.95, $25.00. "SALAMINA" (below), individually hand-painted under the glaze. Gift Package $10.95, $18.95, $32.50.

DON BLANDING'S two new designs, (above) "CORAL REEF"; (below, shown with Gift Package) "HAWAIIAN FLOWERS". In maroon, light blue, pink, light orange. Gift Package $8.95, $15.95, $25.00.

"ULTRA CALIFORNIA" (left). Rich halftones in carnation, aster, gardenia, buttercup. Gift Package, $5.95, $9.50 and $14.95.

Distinction
FOR YOUR TABLE

VERNON'S convenient Gift Package can now be had in three sizes...service for four, service for six, service for eight...at prices shown above. In these sets or in open stock, Vernonware is sold by leading department and home furnishing stores. For color-illustrated booklet showing many beautiful patterns, write Vernon Kilns, Dept. 21, 2300 East 52nd St., Los Angeles, California.

HOW EXQUISITE !" is your inevitable reaction when you first see Vernonware, noting with delight the simple beauty of solid colors, brilliant or pastel . . . the distinctive charm of patterns designed by such gifted artists as Rockwell Kent and Don Blanding.

"How delicate !" you will exclaim when you lift a graceful piece of Vernonware, feel its smooth perfection of texture and note its light weight, a sure indication of fine quality.

"How wonderful !" will be your verdict when you discover that this beautiful, delicate ware is durable enough for constant daily use, and that its glaze is guaranteed not to craze.

For wedding, anniversary or Christmas presents for those friends who appreciate lovely things, or to bring distinction to your own table, choose the ideal gift . . . a set of Vernonware.

Authentic California VERNONWARE

1939 Vernonware advertisement.

Vernon Plaid advertisement featuring "Organdie--bright yellow and warm brown; Gingham--deep green, chartreuse and gay yellow; Homespun-- sunny yellow, rust and deep green; Tam-O-Shanter--forest green border with lime, forest green and cinnamon plaid."

Vernon Kilns Winchester '73 plate, creamer and sugar, dinner plate.

Winchester '73 back stamp.

SHELLEY WINTERS
Starring in "WINCHESTER '73"
A Universal-International Picture

Winchester '73 ... All the romance of the winning of the West, with bold western scenes in dramatic colors on a soft green background. WINCHESTER '73 will tie in with tremendous studio promotion of the great new Universal-International film of the same name.

LOS ANGELES • CALIFORNIA

Promotional advertisement for the movie *Winchester '73* featuring movie actress, Shelley Winters, and Vernon Kilns Winchester '73 dinnerware. *China, Glass & Decorative Accessories*, July 1950.

Brock of California

B.J. Brock and Company, Inc., of Lawndale, California, was incorporated in the state of California from December 29, 1947 to August 29, 1980.

In the past, information on the B.J. Brock Company has been scarce, but through the generosity of Bert J. Brock, we are now able to provide the following information: B.J. Brock & Co. was organized by Bert J. Brock in Lawndale, California in 1947.

Brock, a Dartmouth college graduate, began his ceramic career designing and distributing pottery in Ohio.

After moving to the West Coast with his wife, Amy, Brock purchased a ceramic plant in Lawndale, California, and commenced manufacturing dinnerware under the trade name BROCK of CALIFORNIA. The company's first major dinnerware pattern was California Rustic, a semivitreous ovenware and tableware featuring extra large dinner plates, casseroles, and serving dishes in deep turquoise blue, with a brown "drip" edging. California Rustic dinnerware gave the company national recognition and offices were established in Los Angeles, San Francisco, and subsequently in Chicago, Dallas, and New York.

Brock next introduced Desert Mist, which featured California desert colors, to the solid color market.

This was followed by the company's major entree into the American dinnerware market: California Farmhouse, hand decorated with colorful farm and provincial scenes featuring coupe shaped plates, unusual serving pieces, old-fashioned frying skillets, milk can salt/peppers, butter servers like flat irons on trivets, cauldrons for sugar/creamers, country styled pitchers and lazy susans.

Row 1: Brock California Farmhouse line cup and saucer, coffee server (lid missing), platter. Row 2: Small plate, egg cup, platter, salt and pepper, bowl.

The company's next important pattern, Manzanita, designed for formal dining, featured a new oval shaped plate and serving pieces decorated on a white background with platinum, pink and charcoal decorations.

The above, of course, are only a few of the many popular patterns manufactured by B.J. Brock & Co.

The Brock kiddie set (see section on children's feeding dishes) is identified as the Country Lane pattern. The set was also available in the California Farmhouse pattern.

Advertisement featuring Brock Manzanita.

Catalina Pottery

Mr. William Wrigley, Jr., of Wrigley chewing gum fame, bought Catalina Island in 1919 as a hobby for his retirement. He also envisioned providing those who lived on the island with year-round employment.

The story, as told in Catalina publicity clippings, was that Mr. Wrigley backed his car into a hill on the island and not only became stuck, but was struck with the idea of using the plastic-like clay in pottery.

In the late 1920s Mr. Wrigley opened a pottery plant on the island that produced dinnerware, bowls, vases, lamp bases and other items to sell to visiting tourists. He was quoted in a 1949 magazine article as saying, "I want a bit of Catalina to go to every part of the globe." Indeed it has.

In an attempt to appeal to the tourist trade and to enlist help correcting problems with the island's brittle clay, Mr. Wrigley began to import artisans and potters from the mainland in 1930. After 1930, they began to import clay from the mainland.

The Clay Products Division of Catalina Pottery produced clay tiles and other building products. These were primarily for use on the island.

Catalina Pottery was sold in 1937 to Gladding, McBean & Co. They closed the island pottery at that time. Gladding, McBean & Co. continued to manufacture products using the Catalina molds until 1941.

Shown is a 1937 advertisement for the Catalina Pottery Rancho pattern manufactured by Gladding, McBean & Co. In 1947, Gladding, McBean & Co. returned the rights to the Catalina name to its owner.

Variety of Catalina Island pieces. *Pieces provided courtesy of Laurie and Allan Carter. Photography by Ed Dunn.*

Chicken of the Sea

Both tuna bakers and the plates (shown) were made for the Van Camp's Sea Food Company, Inc. As yet, I have found no information concerning the manufacturer of these pieces other than that they were made in California.

According to a 1941 magazine advertisement, the white fish plate was designed by Inez Donov. The plate has a very soft matte glaze that makes the scales on the fish prominent. The plate is marked "Chicken of the Sea, Made in California."

The tuna bakers may have been made by another manufacturer for Van Camp. They have very high glazes, quite different from the plates, and are incised rather than stamped "Chicken of the Sea." The small shakers are also incised. The tuna baker set came in four colors: Turquoise Blue, Sea Green, Dusky Rose, and Canary Yellow. This set is complete with its own chrome holders "to protect your table and linens from heat."

Chicken of the Sea tuna bakers and plates.

Styled by
INEZ DONOV
10" SIZE

GENUINE *California Pottery*

1941 advertisement showing tuna plate.

Individual **TUNA BAKER & SALAD SERVER**
COLORFUL *California* HAND MADE *Pottery*
WITH SEPARATE CHROME METAL STAND OR COASTER

COLOR CHART

How *you* can get these very *smart* new individual Tuna Bakers is told *in folder on top of every* can of Chicken of the Sea Brand and White Star Brand Tuna—

They are obtainable in your favorite colors of Turquoise Blue, Sea Green, Dusky Rose and Canary Yellow.

Each casserole has a chrome metal stand or coaster to protect your table and linens from heat.

Copy of original Chicken of the Sea brochure.

Flintridge China Company

The Flintridge China Company was started in Pasadena, California in 1946 by Thomas Hogan and Milton Mason. Both men were experienced potters who began with a small kiln and the intentions of producing demitasse cups. They soon expanded to tea pots and then to full china dinnerware sets. They did, with color on china, what the other California plants were doing with earthenware. Their early colors were Laguna Blue, Sunland Yellow and Monterey Coral. Flintridge China Company was incorporated in 1948.

Floyd W. McKee, in his book *The World's Second Oldest Profession, A Century of American Dinnerware,* says that

"Flintridge was started for the manufacture of thin china using a high nepheline syenite body maturing at cone 7." He went on to say that Flintridge's volume (in 1966) had reached 3 1/2 million dollars. Flintridge China Company, Inc., was sold to Gorham Silver in 1970. Flintridge China Company, Inc., was dissolved at that time.

I did not have any Flintridge pieces to photograph but I do have a few advertisements. A finer quality china, Flintridge seems to be a worthwhile investment for collectors.

Gift Suggestions

SWEET 'N LOVELY
Sugar & Creamer $12.50

THE SPICE OF LIFE
Salt & Pepper $3.50

GRACIOUS GIFT
Coffee Server, 6-cup $12.50

If it's fine...it's
Flintridge China

Snow Tulip

...the timeless beauty of a graceful tracery of snow-white tulips on a wide pastel-tint border. Fine, translucent china, finished in sparkling platinum... the ultimate in elegance. Color borders in Grey, sage Green, Cocoa, Blue, Pink.
$15.50 a 5-piece place setting.

Visit us at the shows to see other exciting *new* patterns as well as these Flintridge favorites:

Chalice	Delrose & Marlys	Star Flower
Cocoa Rose	Milan	Sylvan
Continental White	Miramar	Valinda Leaf
Conversation	Santana	Verde
	Sarita	

FLINTRIDGE CHINA CO., 350-380 South Raymond, Pasadena 1, California

Trade publication featuring Flintridge China Co.'s Snow Tulip pattern.

1952 trade publication featuring Miramar pattern.

1952 trade publication featuring Damask Leaf pattern.

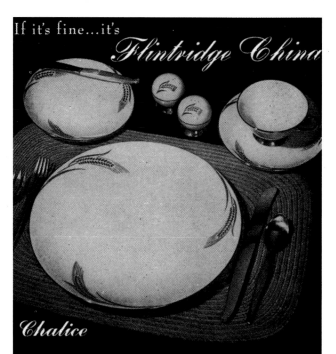

1952 trade publication featuring Chalice pattern.

1952 trade publication featuring Star Flower pattern.

Santa Anita Pottery

Santa Anita Pottery was started about 1939 featuring solid colors in its first ware. Soon thereafter it was purchased by National Silver Company. According to Floyd McKee, the pottery was managed by Mrs. Gertrude Gilkey in Los Angeles, California.

About 1949, Santa Anita Pottery produced a line called California Modern and was still included in their advertisements in 1954 along with the Stylized Spirals, Countryside, Bali Hi, Mayan, Provincial Apple, California Festival and California Rancho patterns.

A 1952 ad has a picture of "Vreni, Santa Anita's top stylist, creator of Vreniware." Vreni's designs included Stylized Spirals, Provincial Apple, Provincial Spiral, Spiral Grape and Provincial Mallard. Santa Anita also made pepper mills, salt and peppers and Lazy Susans.

I have found no information concerning Santa Anita ware after 1954.

California Rancho

California Festival

Provincial Apple

Mayan

Bali-Hi

Countryside

1950s trade publication featuring Santa Anita Ware.

1950s trade publication featuring Santa Anita Ware.

Provincial Mallard

FIRST CHOICE
of fashion editors

FIRST CHOICE
of buyers

FIRST CHOICE
of consumers

Spiral Grape

Vreniware*

*Copyright

FIRST
IN SALES
FOR YOU

VRENI — talented
Swiss designer,
Santa Anita's top
stylist, Creator of
Vreniware*

Provincial Spiral

Santa Anita
Ware
MADE IN CALIFORNIA

Provincial Apple

NEW PATTERNS . . . NEW GLAZES . . . NEW LAZY SUSANS . . .
NEW PROMOTIONS . . . NEW SALES AIDS . . .

santa anita ware
MADE IN CALIFORNIA
3117 San Fernando Rd., Los Angeles 65

A DIVISION OF NATIONAL SILVER COMPANY

Stylized Spirals

Southern California Ceramics Company

Southern California Ceramics Company was started in 1938 when the California Art Products Company was founded by William Guernsey. A move to Santa Monica, California, about 1943 prompted the name change from California Art Products to Southern California Ceramics Company.

Like many other California pottery plants, Southern California's formula was based on talc and "some 50 other ingredients." Their dinnerware line was marketed as Orchard Dinnerware.

ANNOUNCING
THE NEW
Orange Blossom
FROM
CALIFORNIA

Created by SOUTHERN CALIFORNIA CERAMIC COMPANY of Santa Monica

1947 trade publication featuring Southern California Ceramic Co. Orange Blossom pattern.

Mandalay

AN OUTSTANDING Orchard DINNERWARE PATTERN

*An exotic design in white, black and pink
color combinations — bordered in black.*

16 pc. STARTER SERVICE for 4—$14.95 retail

*Now available for shipment in 4 to 6 weeks
after receipt of order.*

F.O.B. CALABASAS, CALIF.

Manufactured by

CALIFORNIA CERAMICS

Sole Selling Agent

NEWLAND, SCHNEELOCH & PIEK, INC.

1107 BROADWAY, NEW YORK 10, N.Y.

NORITAKE WILL NOT BE DISPLAYED AT ANY SHOW

1950s trade publication featuring California Ceramics Mandalay pattern.

The Wallace China Company

Little information is found concerning the Wallace China Company except that it was located in Los Angeles, California, as early as 1931. The company made vitrified restaurant china and is best known for their Westward Ho line. (See section on Best of Western Ware).

The Wallace China Company was purchased by Shenango China Company, New Castle, Pennsylvania, in 1959. The California incorporation was issued on April 10, 1952 and suspended on November 1, 1978. The company had been out of business since the mid 1960s. Shenango China Company closed November 1991.

The Wallace China Company made a very durable restaurant/hotel china. When found, it is usually in excellent condition.

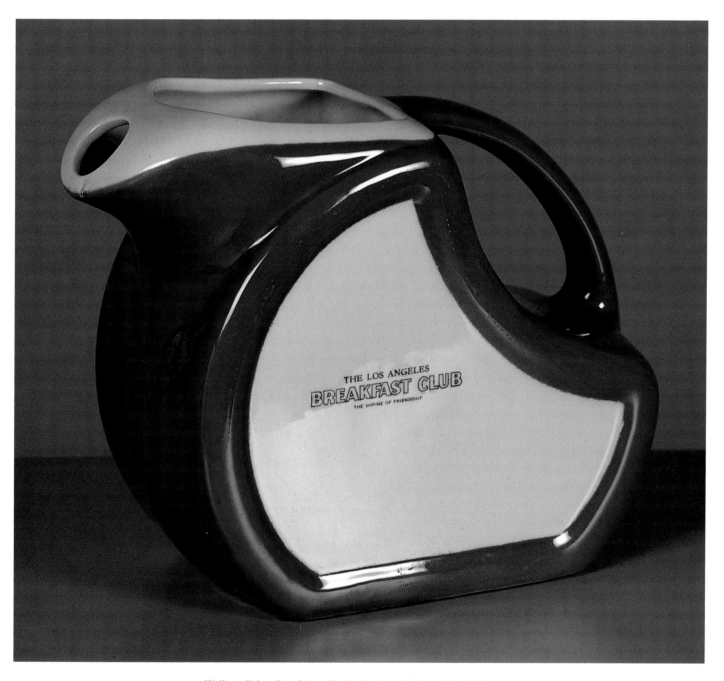

Wallace China Co. pitcher for the Los Angeles Breakfast Club.

Max Weil of California

Max Weil founded the California Figurine Company in 1939. Strong and continued growth under the direction of Larry Pendroy soon created a need for expansion of the plant. The California Figurine Company expanded from 500 square feet in 1939 to 12,000 square feet in 1944. In 1945, another major addition to the plant was completed. Also in that year, the California Figurine Company purchased the Catalina Art Pottery line from Gladding, McBean & Co. The name, California Figurine Company, was then changed to Max Weil of California. Max Weil of California was incorporated in 1948.

The Malay Bambu pattern was their entrance into the dinnerware field; however, Max Weil of California made figurines and many items other than dinnerware.

Max Weil died in 1954, and Frederick Grant took over the Weil Company. The corporation was dissolved in 1960.

Max Weil of California: Dawn Bambu creamer, sugar, platter, shaker.

Hand Decorated MALAY BAMBU

Copyright 1946

Three Beautiful Color Combinations
Meet Every Color Harmony Preference

Coral *Bambu*·Yellow Stalks, Green Leaves, with a Coral Band

Aqua *Bambu*·Black Stalks, White Leaves, on an Aqua Background

and the new

Dawn *Bambu*·Yellow Stalks, Green Leaves, with a Dawn Gray Band

ON DISPLAY AT THE PITTSBURG SHOW—AND AT ALL OTHER MAJOR SHOWS

MAX WEIL OF CALIFORNIA

3160 SAN FERNANDO ROAD   •   LOS ANGELES 41, CALIFORNIA

FIGURINES • DINNERWARE • VASES AND BOWLS

Late 1940s trade publication featuring Malay Bambu.

M.C. Wentz Company

M.C. Wentz was not itself a china or pottery company but a very successful sales operation. Mr. Wentz began his sales company in the midst of the great depression with "$400 and a second-hand automobile." The Wentz Company is best known to collectors for distributing Wallace China Company's Westward Ho line designed by Tillman Goodan.

In 1946, Till Goodan was the art director for the M.C. Wentz Company of Pasadena, California. The company produced many items designed by Till Goodan and his daughter, Betty. Goodan designs included a Horseshoe woodenware knife holder, wooden serving trays, Horseshoe tray feedbox, Ranch Gate napkin holder, Horseshoe tray mounted with Crax-M-All nutcracker in either Ranch Brand or Mountain design, wooden cowboy boots salt and pepper plus many other wooden salt and pepper sets, not in a Western motif.

A search for a California incorporation for the M.C. Wentz Company was not successful but M.C. Wentz was found in the city directories in Colorado Springs, Colorado, in 1955 and 1956. The M.C. Wentz Company was also listed in the 1956 state of Colorado business directory. The Wentz operation was listed in the Colorado directory as a variety and specialty store dealing in oil paintings, pottery and keys.

THE M. C. WENTZ PLANT, PASADENA, CALIFORNIA

Winfield Pottery Company

The Winfield Pottery Company was founded by Lesley Winfield Sample in 1929. Margaret M. Gabriel, a potter and designer, was Sample's partner. After Lesley Sample's death in 1939, Mrs. Gabriel and her husband took over the management of the pottery company. The company expanded rapidly after they assumed management and their line of porcelain dinnerware soon grew to over 400 shapes.

The American Ceramics Company purchased the manufacturing rights to some of the Winfield products in 1946. The ware that came from The American Ceramics Company was incised or marked Winfield or Winfield China. The original Winfield Pottery continued to make china but their products were called Gabriel and will be found incised Gabriel-Pasadena.

A 1950s advertisement from a *Good Housekeeping* magazine offers "An exciting Winfield China invitation" and pictures

actress Jeanne Crain serving coffee from a table filled with Winfield China. The Winfield China Company also offered a written 100-year replacement against defects, chipping, cracking or breakage. The ad also states "Your pattern will always be permanently available. . . . It is guaranteed to be oven proof . . . Will not fade or craze. Your investment in Winfield is protected." The small print concerning the replacement guarantee reads "Replaced free for the 1st year and at 1/2 price for the next 99 years." A coupon was also included inviting customers to write for information to show them how to order Winfield China direct from the factory "for as little as $10 a month."

The Winfield China Company was incorporated in the state of California on February 20, 1959, as Winfield China Company, Inc. That incorporation was terminated in October 1969.

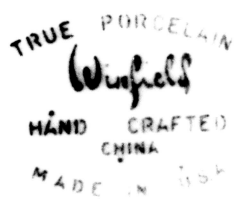

Winfield Ware: Bamboo pattern color advertisement from ladies' magazine.

Winfield China (pattern unknown).

Winfield China (pattern unknown).

Winfield Pottery: Gabriel platter (pattern unknown).

TAHOE, with choice of square (10″, $3.25) or round (10″, $3) plates and cups and saucers (square, $3.25; round, $3) has white background, brown rim, brown pinecones and blue-green spray, handpainted underglaze. 5-pc. setting, $9.50, $10.50, Gabriel.

Trade publication featuring Gabriel's Tahoe pattern.

WINFIELD DRAGON FLOWER pattern in beige, pink, and dark brown motif on white background; now being shown in 34 different shapes by American Ceramic Products, Inc., 1825 Sanford Street, Santa Monica, Cal.

1948 Trade publication featuring Winfield's Dragon Flower pattern.

Collecting children's feeding dishes is an exciting adventure. While most children's pieces originally came in sets, the collector seldom finds these pieces in sets. Collectors are buying whatever pieces they can find to assemble them into sets.

Don't be misled by the decal or decoration when putting sets together. Shapes, the weight of the ware, handle shapes and background glazes are all better guidelines to matching sets. As you can see from the photographs of children's feeding dishes, the same decorations were used by several different companies.

Children's dishes come in a variety of shapes, glaze colors and decorations. Some decals are whimsical. Some are favorite characters from nursery rhymes, movies and television shows. Some decals on the earlier pieces are frightening.

At some point in time, most American pottery-china companies made children's feeding dishes. The pieces represented here are just a few of the many children's dishes yet to be found by some fortunate collector.

Children's pieces of all kinds have long been sought out by collectors. Consider yourself fortunate if you find children's pieces in mint condition. It is not an easy feat, nor is it inexpensive, but as in all areas of collecting, bargains can be found from time to time.

Row 1: Harker Cameoware - "Pink Bunny" bowl; "Parasol" Cameoware plate; "Circus" mug. Row 2: Continental Kilns - "Blue Lamb" mug; "Ducky" plate and bowl. (The intaglio design is much deeper in the Harker pieces.)

Row 1: Crooksville China Co. - Raggedy Ann and Andy plate, mug and divided dish (copyright 1941 Johnny Gruelle); Harker - "Spot" plate and mug. Row 2: Crooksville China Co. - Raggedy Ann and Andy bowl; Homer Laughlin China Co. - (made for Ralston Purina Co.) "Um-m All Gone" bowl; Unmarked - "Marching Bears" unusual two-handled mug; Unmarked - "Piggy Picnic" mug (copyright Tom Lamb); Company unknown - Rudolph the Red Nose Reindeer (copyright R.L.M.) Robert L. May, originator of the Rudolph character; Sebring Pottery Co. Uncle Wiggily mug, made for Wander Co., makers of Ovaltine.

Rudolph the Red Nose Reindeer plate - Company unknown, (copyright R.L.M.) Robert L. May, originator of the Rudolph character.

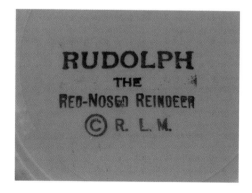

Backstamp as it appears on Rudolph the Red Nose Reindeer plate.

Row 1: Knowles, Taylor and Knowles China Co. - Little Boy Blue plate; Steubenville China Co. - Little Miss Muffet pitcher. Row 2: All U.S. Pottery Co. - "House That Jack Built" plate; "This is the House" pitcher or creamer; "This is the Man" cup and saucer.

Winfield China Co. Tender Age three piece child's set. Set consists of 8" plate, cereal bowl and 8 oz. mug.

Wee Modern three piece child's set. Designed by Eva Zeisel.

Row 1: Taylor, Smith and Taylor - Howdy Doody plate and mug; "Three Little Pigs" divided dish, plate and mug. Row 2: Homer Laughlin China Co. - Unmarked Dick Tracy bowl; Unmarked Little Orphan Annie mug; Sebring China Co. (under Patriot China mark for Walt Disney Enterprises) Donald Duck mug; Universal Potteries - Beauregard and Elsie mugs; Continental Kilns - Elsie mug.

Row 1: Company unknown - marked Fox's Credit Jewelers, "There Was an Old Woman" heavy ware yellow glaze plate; Crown Potteries - "Chickie-Two" divided plate and mug, red loop border; Company unknown - marked Roma, "This is the Cat" divided plate, very heavy ware. Row 2: Edwin M. Knowles China Co. - "Darlin' Doggy" cup and bowl; All Unmarked - "Patches" mug; "Tea Party" mug; "The Musicians" mug; W.S. George China Co. - "First Love" mug, signed by G.G. Drayton; "Playtime" plate.

Southern Potteries three piece child set, hand decorated, as advertised in *China, Glass & Accessories*, January, 1953.

Row 1: Homer Laughlin China Co. - "I Go Here" plate, Betsy McCall and Nosy; Shenango China Co. - "Little Bo Peep" mug; Homer Laughlin China Co. - "I Go Here" plate "Dinnertime"; Unmarked - "Beggin" mug; Homer Laughlin China Co. - "I Go Here" plate "Mr. Bear's Dinner". All "I Go Here" plates shown are made by Homer Laughlin China Co. for International Silver Co. and come boxed with fork and spoon, 1950's. Row 2: Unmarked - "Baby Chick" heavy mug; Company unknown - "Mary Had a Little Lamb" plate, advertising piece for Vance Furniture; Unmarked - "Little Boy Blue" mug; Unmarked - Little Jack Horner plate; Unmarked - "Hunter" mug; Unmarked - "See Saw" plate; W.S. George Pottery Co. - "Castles" mug; Company unknown - "Carousel" plate, advertising piece for Ash Furniture; Company unknown - "Hankscraft" blue mug.

1953 advertisement for "I Go Here" plates. One plate is decorated with Betsy McCall and the other plate is Jimmy Weeks. Betsy McCall's silverware is Romance and Jimmy Weeks' silverware is May Queen.

Row 1: Unmarked - "Giving Thanks" plate and mug; Crown Pottery Co. - "Skating Monkey" mug and bowl set; Edwin M. Knowles China Co. - "Patches" mug; Universal Potteries-"Three Bears" plate and mug. Row 2: Salem China Co. "Little Boy Blue" divided bowl; Company unknown - "Asleep in the Hay" mug, advertising piece for Gustafson Furniture Store, San Diego; Company unknown - "Little Bo Peep" mug, advertising piece for Miles Furniture Co., Corsicana, Texas; Unmarked - "Hickory Dickory Dock" mug; Company unknown - "See Saw" mug, advertising piece for Clark and Eoff Stores, Harrison, Arkansas; Universal Potteries - "Three Bears" bowl (goes with mug and plate directly above on Row 1).

Row 1: Homer Laughlin China Co. - "Campfire" plate on Rhythm shape, 1952; Unmarked - "Elves" plate, cup and saucer; Taylor, Smith and Taylor - "Tricks" plate on Iona shape; Dora of California - Lil Miss Muffet milk pitcher. Row 2: Jackson China Co. "Fox Goes A'Courtin" plate; Mayer China Co. "Playtime" plate; Syracuse China Co. "Dutch Friends" plate and bowl.

Row 1: All Roseville Pottery Co. - mini cup and saucer, creamer, milk pitcher. Row 2: All Roseville Pottery Co. - small plate, bowl, plate.

November 1949 advertisement from *China, Glass & Decorative Accessories* featuring Roseville's juvenile line with different decals.

Wallace China Co. Little Buckaroo set (mug missing).

Little Buckaroo backstamp.

Little Buckaroo set as shown in 1950s advertisement from W.C. Wentz Co.

Hall China Co. - "Little Bo Peep" divided feeding dish, chicken stopper. Sold through Christmas Jewel 1954 catalog. It was also available through other sources.

Hall China Co. - "Animal Friends" divided feeding dish. *Photo by Keith Carey.*

Row 1: All Stangl China Co. - Little Boy Blue plate; Cow in the Meadow bowl. Row 2: All Stangl China Co. - Our Barnyard Friends mug, divided feeding dish, mug.

Stangl China Co. - Mealtime Special feeding set.

Row 1: Unmarked - "Tea Party" set, cup and saucer, creamer, teapot and plate (sugar not shown). Row 2: Jackson China Co. - restaurant ware, Chicken mug; W.S. George China Co. - "Friends" plate on Bolero shape.

1950s Kiddie Set by Brock of California - salad plate, bowl, available in Country Lane (shown) and the California Farmhouse patterns. The Brock Kiddie Set was priced to sell at $3.95 per set.

Row 1: All Edwin Knowles China Co. - "Tea Party" set, "Wheat" sugar, creamer, teapot, plate, cup and saucer. Row 2: All Edwin Knowles China Co. - "Flower Pots" plate, saucer, different style teapot and creamer.

Roy Rogers

5-piece Children's Set

Designed by Roy Rogers. His own way of bringing "many happy trails" to young ones at meal-time. Colorful figures of Roy and Trigger make youngsters feel they're right on the corral fence. Set includes 7-oz. mug, 6½-in. cereal soup, 5-in. sauce dish, 6¼-in. plate, 9¼-in. plate. Ivory color semi-porcelain
35 E 04692—Shpg. wt. 3 lbs.........5-pc. Set **$2.79**

Opposite Page:
1921 *China, Glass & Lamps* featuring Hold-Fast and No-Splash baby plates.

1950 *Sears Catalog* featuring five piece children's set. Designed by Roy Rogers.

Suggestions

Hold-Fast Baby Plate

FOR FALL
FOR CHRISTMAS

Tea Party Sets (26 Piece) at $2 to $2.50 a Set

A B C Plates   at $21 to $24 a gross

Baby Plates   Hold Fast and No-Splash

Salads and Cakes   at $24 to $60 a gross

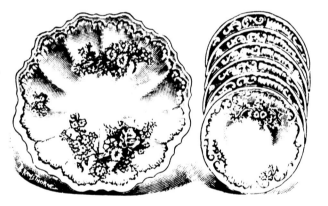

Berry Sets   *Game Sets*

Cake Sets   *Fish Sets*

Cottage Dinner Sets

Make

Practical and Beautiful
Christmas Presents

———

No-Splash Baby Plate

The D. E. McNicol Pottery Co.
EAST LIVERPOOL, OHIO

Chapter Five: The Best of The Designers

The designers mentioned in this section have backgrounds as varied as writer, ceramist, artist, dancer, and industrial designer. From these varied artistic backgrounds came the inspiration for a myriad of dinnerware lines appreciated and collected throughout the country.

Don Blanding

Don Blanding was born in Kingfisher, Oklahoma, on November 7, 1894. His father was a lawyer and a judge. When land was given to settlers, his family relocated to Lawton, Oklahoma. His early sketches were of Indians and his school books were covered with them. The very first earnings from his drawings were his sketches of Indian heads on leather.

He worked one summer in Yellowstone Park and continued on to the Chicago Art Institute from 1913 to 1915. He took a job as an usher at a theater in order to pay his way through art school. While working at the theater in 1915, he saw the play *The Bird of Paradise*. The play inspired him to pack up and move in one short week to Hawaii.

Mr. Blanding did many things while in Hawaii. He lived among the native people, explored the dead crater of Haleakala and listened to the legends of the people. Many of his characters came from his Hawaiian experiences.

After studying art in Paris and London, he worked as a commercial artist, cartoonist, copy writer and eventually became an author. His first book was *Leaves From a Grass House*. Three publishers rejected it and he published it jointly with the *Honolulu Star Bulletin*.

Mr. Blanding headed for California. He built his "Vagabond's House" in Hollywood which he furnished with cushions in the true Hawaiian tradition. During his California stay, he designed and executed a mural border for the Hotel Huntington in Pasadena which is thought to be one of his best works.

Don Blanding was commissioned to design dinnerware for Vernon Kilns. His designs reflect his love for Hawaii in the patterns Coral Reef, Hawaiian Flowers, Lei Lani and others. An accomplished author, illustrator, lecturer, traveler, Don Blanding's favorite saying was, "The trick of doing a thing well is knowing where to start."

He always began and ended his letters with "Aloha" and somewhere in every letter that he wrote, he inserted a small sketch of a mynah bird. He died in 1957.

Designer Don Blanding.

Vernon Kilns Leilani pattern designed by Don Blanding.

Surf Ballet pattern designed by Sascha Brastoff.

Sascha Brastoff

Sascha Brastoff was born on October 23, 1918, in Cleveland, Ohio, to Louis and Rebecca Brastoff and was educated at the Cleveland School of Art in Cleveland, Ohio.

Sascha Brastoff was truly a multi-talented artist. He was a ballet dancer at the Cleveland Ballet in the 1930s, a sculptor and designer of costumes for 20th Century Fox, a sergeant in the United States Army, and a member of the cast of "Winged Victory" when it went to Hollywood. In 1946, he was awarded the Syracuse Ceramic Award and in 1947, Sascha Brastoff Products, Incorporated, came to be.

Winthrop Rockefeller was very impressed with Sascha Brastoff's abilities as a ceramist and backed him financially in a factory in 1948. That factory suffered a devastating fire in 1952. Mr. Rockefeller once again backed him after the fire and a new plant opened in 1953, covering an entire west Los Angeles block with 35,000 square feet at a cost of $500,000.

The dedication of the opening at the new plant was a gala Hollywood style event with over 1,000 guests attending. Zsa Zsa Gabor, Mitzi Gaynor and Edward G. Robinson were on hand to help Mr. Brastoff dedicate the plant.

The new Sascha Brastoff plant had a "glass-walled" gallery displaying Mr. Brastoff's work. For the opening more than 200 Brastoff pieces were on loan from galleries in Houston and New York City. The plant operated until 1973.

Sascha Brastoff designed for other companies as well. In 1968, he designed Blue Spruce for the Winfield China Company and between 1970-1972 he designed a line of lamps and ashtrays for the Haeger Potteries in Illinois.

Exhibits of Sascha Brastoff's work were held at the Los Angeles County Museum and others. In his later years, he designed jewelry and produced holograms. Sascha Brastoff passed away February 4, 1993.

Sascha Brastoff backstamp.

BLUE SPRUCE, designed by Sascha Brastoff for Winfield China; hand-decorated, ovenproof and vitrified. 16-piece set retails for $14.95. American Ceramic Products, Inc., Santa Monica, Cal.

Reprint of Blue Spruce pattern designed by Sascha Brastoff.

Sascha Brastoff

From sculptured decorative accessories to fabulous translucent china, the thrill of discovering Sascha Brastoff creations is matched only by the joy of owning them. For collectors of Sascha B. signed originals, this is a "vintage year."

ceramics — lamps — fine china

SASCHA BRASTOFF PRODUCTS, INC.
11520 W. Olympic Blvd., Los Angeles 64
New brochure H-1, 25¢

1950s advertisement picturing Sascha Brastoff.

Tillman Parker Goodan

Tillman Parker Goodan was born in Eaton, Colorado, on March 27, 1896. He spent his early years in Colorado and both his love of horse riding and drawing were evident early on although he had very little formal training in either one.

While still a young boy, Mr. Goodan moved to the small farm in California where he lived most of his life. It was at a neighboring ranch that he gained skills as a calf roper and cowboy. By the 1930s, he was beginning to receive recognition for his western art, and by the early 1940s, he and his daughter, Betty, were illustrating comic books for his longtime friend, Gene Autry. Betty was also a world champion cowgirl.

During the late 1940s, a wholesale company purchased two of Mr. Goodan's paintings to display at a trade show. The Goodan paintings created so much interest that arrangements were made to meet with the artist. The Westward Ho dinnerware designed by Mr. Goodan was a result of this meeting. Westward Ho was made by the Wallace China Company of Los Angeles and distributed by the M.C. Wentz Sales Organization.

On May 24, 1958, at the Tulare California Rodeo, while waiting astride his horse for his introduction in the Grand Entry, Till Goodan suffered a fatal heart attack. He was 62 years old. In an article that appeared in the magazine *Corral Dust*, Fall 1964, Vol. 9, Number 4, it was said, "At 62 he died as he might have wished, actively participating in a life he knew and loved."

Serious collectors seek out all of Till Goodan's work--not just the Westward Ho designed dinnerware lines. Till Goodan was a versatile artist whose love for the rodeo and the west was reflected in all of his work. Western decorated tablecloths, ties, prints, calendars, postcards and paintings make up the wide variety of collectibles designed by Till Goodan.

Tillman Goodan

Till Goodan's work is being recreated once again by his daughter, Betty Goodan Andrews, who retains sole control of the rights to her father's name and all of his work. Mrs. Andrews has licensed Jacob Roberts Inc. of Los Angeles to produce silk neckties copied from twelve original patterns from the 1940s. Three other companies have been licensed by Mrs. Andrews to recreate Till Goodan's western art.

Westward Ho 13" salad bowl.

Rockwell Kent

Rockwell Kent lived life to its fullest and his art reflected his virility and spirit. It has been said of Kent that "he escaped into the wilderness" and his art is self-explanatory.

Mr. Kent was born on June 21, 1982. He began art classes and then studied architecture at Columbia University. About 1905, he visited Monhegan Island where he worked as a lobsterman and driller. He also painted while he was there.

Mr. Kent went to Newfoundland for a time and on his return in 1916 he incorporated as Rockwell Kent, Inc., to raise enough money for him to depart for Alaska in 1918. In 1920, he moved to Vermont where his first book, *Wilderness,* was published. *Wilderness* contains several illustrations of his trip to Alaska.

In 1928, Mr. Kent went to Denmark and Greenland. In 1935, he wrote *Salamina,* a book based on his Alaskan experiences. In the 1930s, Vernon Kilns commissioned him to design decorations for their Vernon Kilns dinnerware. He designed three dinnerware sets for Vernon Kilns: Moby Dick, Salamina and Our America. These lines did not prove to be as popular as anticipated and much was returned to the company.

Rockwell Kent was an illustrator, painter, print maker and author. He illustrated other author's books, among them *Moby Dick, Beowulf,* and *The Canterbury Tales.* It is only fitting that collectors have treasured any pieces of Kent's Vernon Kilns ware as the true art it is.

His works were rejected by an American museum in 1960 (probably due to Joseph McCarthy's interest in Kent's possible Communist activities) and he donated the rejected works to the Soviet Union. He received the Lenin Peace Prize in 1967 and died in New York on March 13, 1971, at the age of 89.

Rockwell Kent

Vernon Kilns Salamina pattern large plate and tumbler.

1939 Vernonware advertisement showing Don Blanding's and Rockwell Kent's designs.

Iroquois Butterfly ashtray designed by Peter Max, part of the Cliff Dweller line.

Peter Max

Peter Max was born in Germany in 1937. He came to the United States with his family in 1953 and studied at the Art Students League, the Pratt Graphics Art Center and the School of Visual Arts in New York City.

In 1967, the Iroquois China Company introduced the pattern, Love, which was designed by Peter Max. Love was described as a "psychedelic style splashed across" Iroquois China plates, mugs and bowls. The pattern was part of the Iroquois Cliff-Dwellers line in the colors blue, red, yellow and green.

The Butterfly decoration was offered in a 1968 *China, Glass and Tableware* trade magazine as yet another pattern in the Iroquois Cliff-Dwellers line. Butterfly was described as an "art nouveau design" in pink, blue and orange against a taffy brown background.

The Iroquois Cliff-Dwellers group did not escape Mr. Max's flair for design and color. The Peter Max designs are found on fabrics, rugs, posters, tableware, shopping bags, posters and much more.

Trade advertisement for both the Iroquois Love pattern and Butterfly pattern.

BUTTERFLY, with stylized daisies, decorates china plate, mug, and bowl in the new Cliff-Dwellers group designed by Peter Max; the art nouveau design in pink, blue, and orange sparkles against a taffy brown ground. A gift-packed set for two retails for $14.95. The Iroquois China Company.

China, Glass & Tableware 1968 advertisement reprinted with permission of Doctorow Communications, Inc. Clifton, N.J.

THE IROQUOIS CHINA COMPANY. "Love" is splashed across a plate, bowl, and mug in psychedelic style by Peter Max, designer of this unusual new Cliff-Dwellers china line; colors are blue, red, yellow, and green. A packaged service for two retails for $14.95.

Don Schreckengost

Don Schreckengost was born in Sebring, Ohio, to Adda and Warren Schreckengost. All three of the Schreckengost's sons, Viktor, Paul and Don, were destined to become distinguished ceramic designers. Don graduated from Sebring High School and attended the Cleveland Art Institute where he graduated with honors. Stockholm, Sweden, was Don's next stop for "special studies" after which he was a guest instructor in ceramics at Escuela de Bellas Artes in Mexico.

Internationally known as a ceramics designer, Don is a recipient of numerous awards in many mediums of art. These awards included the Award of Merit for Product Design at Artists in Industry Exhibit, First Award for Fine Art Pottery, Contemporary Exhibition of Ceramics of Western Hemisphere, the Menno Alexander Reeb Award for Sculpture (Albright Art Gallery), and the Special Award for Commercial Art (Memorial Art Gallery). He was the sculptor and designer of the Albert Victor Bleininger Bronze Medal and planned and designed the U.S. Exhibition for the U.S. Potters Association National Home Furnishings Show in New York.

A member of many professional and civic organizations, Don Schreckengost served as vice-president of the Ohio chapter of the Industrial Designers Society, chairman of Art and Design committee of the U.S. Potters Association and chairman and trustee of the Design division, American Ceramic Society. He is the co-founder of Little League baseball in East Liverpool, Ohio, and a recipient of the Distinguished Citizens Award.

Many of the familiar dinnerware shapes and patterns that collectors currently seek were designed by Don Schreckengost or his brother, Viktor. Don has designed for the Homer Laughlin China Company, U.S. Stoneware, Mayer China Company, Royal China Company and others. He is currently design director for the Hall China Company and executive design director for Summitville Tile, Inc., Summitville, Ohio.

The Sherlock Holmes teapot (pictured) was designed by Don Schreckengost in 1986. The teapot was a joint effort between Mr. Schreckengost and Dan and Ann Brasier. The Brasiers are avid Hall collectors and the Hall China Company was a preferred choice for their Sherlock Holmes teapot idea. The backstamp has Hall in a circle and the initials "DWB DAS" for Brasier and Schreckengost.

Listed below is a partial listing of Don Schreckengost's dinnerware designs over the years.

1933 Tricorne, Streamline, Salem.
1948 Skytone, sky-blue body.
Suntone-terra cotta.
Rhythm, (solid colors) dark green, yellow, chartreuse, burgundy, gray.
Cavalier.
Epicure.
Duraprint-designs on shape include Daybreak, Dogwood, Brown-eyed Susan, Harvest, Highland Plaid.
Applique-Yellow Daisy and Black-Eyed Susan.
Triumph (a porcelain dinnerware), decorations: Woodland, Pastel Rose, Linda and others.
1950 Debutante-Champagne pattern.
Royal Stone-a stoneware, Royal China.
Royal Cavalier.
Royalyn glassware.
1986 Noel, Salem.

Don has also designed service ware for airlines and Amtrak, and he is a prize-winning restaurant ware designer.

Epicure designed by Don Schreckengost for the Homer Laughlin China Co.

Sherlock Holmes teapot made by Hall China Co. and designed by Don Schreckengost.

"Sailing"

EX5018½—32 Pc. Set _ _ _ _ _ _ - $10.40
EX5018—53 Pc. Set _ _ _ _ _ _ _ 20.40

Unusually smart, this streamlined design is a reproduction of a well-known artist's version of a ship motif. The **coral and black sailboats** with their guiding stars are reminiscent of the bright sails of an old-world fishing fleet. Set off by coral and platinum lined edges.

All Priced

F. O. B. New York

or Factory at Salem, Ohio.

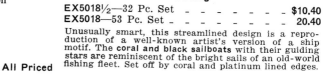

American Dinnerware

"Mandarin Tricorne"

EX5025—24 Pc. Cup-Plate Bridge Set _ _ _ $10.70

The outstanding bridge set of the year with its unusual Tricorne shape and new cup-plate feature. Plates have solid gay red borders, with white interiors. Cups—solid red exterior, white interior. Glasses have gay red stripes. Set consists of 4 cup-plates; 4 cups; 4 beverage glasses; 4 sippers; 4 nut dishes; 1 creamer; 1 sugar and cover (2 pcs.); 1 sandwich tray. This novel set solves the hostess' serving problem and its gay colors add a festive note to any Bridge or Buffet Luncheon or Afternoon Tea.

"Monogram"

EX5015— 35 Pc. Set _ _ _ _ _ _ _ _ _ _ _ - $14.90
EX5016— 53 Pc. Set _ _ _ _ _ _ _ _ _ _ _ 23.10
EX5017—100 Pc. Set _ _ _ _ _ _ _ _ _ _ _ 48.10

The essence of "smartness" is reflected in a dinner table set with monogrammed silver, glassware and dishes. This lovely streamlined pattern is beautifully decorated in 23 karat gold; available with any desired initial. **(Monogrammed Dinnerware is made to order and requires a few extra days for shipping.)**

Bennett Brothers 1938 catalog featuring Don Schreckengost's designs.

Homer Laughlin China Co. Skytone shape designed by Don
Schreckengost.

CROCKERY & GLASS JOURNAL for March

Homer Laughlin China Co. Highland Plaid pattern designed by Don
Schreckengost.

Fifth Avenue

This lovely high-styled pattern—"As New As Tomorrow"—sets
the fashion note in contemporary dinnerware design.
The delicate harlequin motif in crisp, fresh decorator-colors of
turquoise, gray and black makes "FIFTH AVENUE" the first
choice of the sophisticated hostess.

The Homer Laughlin China Co.
NEWELL, WEST VIRGINIA

CROCKERY & GLASS JOURNAL for May, 1955

Homer Laughlin China Co. Fifth Avenue pattern designed by Don
Schreckengost.

American Provincial

Inspired by the timeless art of an earlier century,
Homer Laughlin's designers and skilled craftsmen
created bright, gay and colorful design motifs to
grace the smooth, smart lines of a new contemporary shape to produce "AMERICAN PROVINCIAL."
A truly American dinnerware pattern styled for
today and for tomorrow.

The Homer Laughlin China Co.
NEWELL, WEST VIRGINIA

1951 advertisement from *China, Glass & Decorative Accessories* featuring Homer Laughlin China Co.'s American Provincial.

Homer Laughlin China Co. sales brochure featuring various Epicure pieces.

Opposite Page:
Noel Christmas collection designed by Don Schreckengost and distributed by Salem China Co.

Homer Laughlin China Co., Epicure pattern designed by Don Schreckengost.

The Salem China Co.

Viktor Schreckengost

Viktor Schreckengost

Viktor Schreckengost, Don's brother, was also born in Sebring, Ohio. His parents' families had been potters in Pennsylvania before moving to Sebring.

Mr. Schreckengost attended the Cleveland School of Art. After graduation he studied at the Kuntstgewerbeschule, Vienna, Austria. He returned to Cleveland in 1930 and became a designer for Cowan Pottery and assistant to the pottery's founder, R. Guy Cowan. While at Cowan Pottery, he designed many pieces including the Jazz Bowl which recently sold at auction for $47,000.00. A smaller version of the Jazz Bowl which was originally priced at $25 sold for $28,000 in 1993. He was also an instructor at the Cleveland School of Art.

After the Cowan Pottery closed in 1932, R. Guy Cowan, who had been the head of the Cowan Pottery, became art director and designer for the Syracuse China Company in Syracuse, New York. Viktor designed several patterns for restaurant and hotel ware made at Syracuse.

In 1933, Mr. Schreckengost became a designer for Limoges China Company in Sebring, Ohio. He designed two new shapes, Americana and Diana, for Limoges.

In 1934, Mr. Schreckengost became a designer for Salem China Company. By this time, his work had been exhibited at the Metropolitan Museum of Art, Pennsylvania Museum, Akron Art Institute, Cleveland Museum of Art, Chicago Art Institute and the Syracuse Museum. He continued to design for Sebring and Salem until 1943 when he entered the Navy. After the war, he returned to design for Salem China Company.

During the 1930s and 1940s, he designed many products such as glassware, stoves, furniture, trucks, buses, bicycles, wheelgoods and printing presses.

Viktor Schreckengost went on to do several Terra-Cotta sculptures which won him the Gold Medals, American Institute of Architecture.

Christmas Eve pattern designed by Viktor Schreckengost. Christmas Eve was originally made by the Salem China Co.

Designs and shapes by Viktor Schreckengost include:

AMERICAN LIMOGES
1933   Americana shape-Patterns: Smoke, Flame, Oleander.
      Diana shape-(fluted)-Patterns: Evening Star, Joan of Arc patterns.
1935   Manhattan shape-Patterns: Flower Shop, Santa Fe, Animal Kingdom, Red Sails, Garden of Eden, many banded patterns.
      Snowflake shape (embossed).
1937   Triumph shape-Patterns: Bermuda, Norway, Sweden, various colored band treatments.
1940   Candlelight shape-Patterns: Regency Bouquet, Federal, Old Virginia, National Bouquet.
      Embassy shape.
1942   Jiffy Ware-space saving design (refrigerator/ baking ware), trim in red, blue, yellow, green.

SALEM CHINA CO.
1942   HOTCO Ware (Oven and refrigerator ware), trim in red, blue, yellow, green.
1943   Victory shape-Patterns: Colonial Firesides, Petit Point.
1948   Tempo shape-Patterns: Parsley, Orchard, Lansdowne.
1950   Lotus Bud shape-Patterns: (Far East influence)

Cherry Blossom, Water Lily (eight flowers), shape has short rim, fluted base on holloware.
1951   Ranch shape-Four solid colors, lime yellow, maple red, pine green, birch gray-Patterns on Ranch shape: Melody Lane, Plantation, Geranium, Primrose, Anniversary.
      Flair shape (rounded square)-Patterns:
      Constellation (matte white with dark blue flecks) with accent pieces in Charcoal matte glaze, Good Morning, Jackstraws.
1952   Ranch shape-Sterling Color series: Coral, Green, Gray, Lime, Snow.
      Flair shape (white glaze)-Patterns:
      Peach and Clover.
1955   Free Form shape (Holloware supported on small feet, cup granted first patent for a cup in 100 years for its dripless feature) All items were unusual in form, made in nutmeg glaze with semi-matte and small brown flecks. Most popular pattern-Cave Man: early cave-like drawings of people and animals, in sepia and burnt sienna. Candleholder, black wire trivets were available for keeping casseroles, teapots and coffee servers hot.
1994   Christmas Eve pattern is still being made in many countries and is currently being distributed by Salem China Co.

COMPOSITION OF SETS (For composition of smaller sets see opposite page)

100 Pc. Set *(Shipping Weight 80 lbs.)*

Popular Sized Sets				Cambridge Crystal Glassware Pages 226 and 227
12 Cups	12 Coupe Soups 7"	1 Gravy Boat	1 Covd. Sugar (2 Pcs.)	
12 Saucers	12 Fruits	1 Cheese Plate	1 Covd. Veg. Dish (2 Pcs.)	
12 Dinner Plates 9"	1 Ob. Open Veg. Dish 9"	1 Meat Platter 11"	1 Jelly Bowl	
12 B and B Plates 6"	1 Rd. Open Veg. Dish 8"	1 Meat Platter 13"		
12 Pie Plates 7"	1 Pickle Dish	1 Cream Pitcher	1 Covd. Butter (3 Pcs.)	

Advertisement featuring Victory shape designed by Viktor Schreckengost.

Jiffy Ware designed by Viktor Schreckengost.

MODERN DINNERWARE

Introducing the New VICTORY SHAPE with decorations to enhance its natural beauty.

DINNER SETS SHOWN ON THIS PAGE ARE MADE UP OF THE FOLLOWING PIECES

32-Pc. Set	53-Pc. Set	100-Pc. Set	
6—Cups	8—Dinner Plates 9″	12—Cups	1—Meat Platter 11″
6—Saucers	8—B. & B. Plates 6″	12—Saucers	1—Meat Platter 13″
6—Dinner Plates 9″	8—Coupe Soups 6″	12—Dinner Plates 9″	1—Jelly Bowl
6—B. & B. Plates 6″	8—Fruits	12—Pie Plates 7″	1—Cov. Butter (3 pcs.)
6—Fruits	8—Cups	12—B. & B. Plates 6″	1—Cheese Plate 6″
1—Meat Platter 11″	8—Saucers	12—Coupe Soups 6″	1—Gravy Boat
1—Open Veg. Dish 8″	1—Covd. Sugar (2 pcs.)	12—Fruits	1—Cream Pitcher
	1—Creamer	1—Ob. Open Veg. Dish 9″	1—Covd. Sugar (2 pcs.)
	1—Platter 11″	1—Rd. Open Veg. Dish 8″	1—Covd. Veg. Dish (2 pcs.)
	1—Open Veg. Dish 8″	1—Pickle Dish	

VIENNA DESIGN

ry beautiful pattern, with rose center design, and rose lace border
t. A lovely blue and ivory background helps to bring out the at-
tive colors in this design. The beauty is further enhanced by the
ivory band, which encircles the verge of this ware bordered with
vn lines on each side. This makes a very pretty effect, and shows
o marvelous advantage on the snow-white body of the new Victory
erware, which is of the very latest style and design.

GARDEN DESIGN

A beautiful bouquet of flowers, with red and yellow tulips predominating adorn the center of this ware. A coral line on the verge surrounded
by a heavier grey band which harmonizes with the background of the
center design, giving a final touch to this attractive decoration. The
handles are especially treated in grey and coral. The shape is the new
"Victory" designed by a famous ceramic artist of the Cleveland Art
School. It represents the last word in ceramic designing.

Victory shape dinnerware.

MODERN DINNERWARE
Introducing the New VICTORY SHAPE
with decorations to enhance its natural beauty.

DINNER SETS SHOWN ON THIS PAGE ARE MADE UP OF THE FOLLOWING PIECES

32-Pc. Set:	53-Pc. Set:	100-Pc. Set	
6—Cups	8—Dinner Plates 9″	12—Cups	1—Meat Platter 11″
6—Saucers	8—Bread & Butter Plates 6″	12—Saucers	1—Meat Platter 13″
6—Dinner Plates 9″	8—Coupe Soups 6″	12—Dinner Plates 9″	1—Jelly Bowl
6—Bread & Butter Plates 6″	8—Fruits	12—Pie Plates 7″	1—Cov. Butter (3-pcs.)
6—Fruits	8—Cups	12—B & B Plates 6″	1—Cheese Plate 6″
1—Meat Platter 11″	8—Saucers	12—Coupe Soups 6″	.—Gravy Boat
1—Open Vegetable Dish 8″	1—Covered Sugar (2-pcs.)	12—Fruits	1—Cov. Sugar (2-pcs.)
	1—Creamer	1—Ob. Open Veg. Dish 9″	1—Cream Pitcher
	1—Platter 11″	1—Rd. Open Veg. Dish 8″	1—Covd. Veg. Dish (2-pcs.)
	1—Open Vegetable Dish 8″	1—Pickle Dish	

Doily Petit Point

This "Doily Petit Point" pattern on the new Victory shape is an outstanding contribution to modern designing. This very beautiful pattern embodies all the dignity and grace of rare old lace. The design features a beautiful rose center with a floral border, all worked out in the new Petit Point or cross-stitch design. The handles are all treated with a wide gold bar giving added attractiveness to this decoration. A fawn background adds the final touch to this lovely pattern.

The shape is the new "Victory," designed by a noted ceramic designer of the Cleveland Art School. Surely if you are interested in fine furnishings for that home of yours this beautifully shaped chinaware so smartly decorated will appeal to you. You will find listed below three different size sets, one to meet the requirements of any size family.

NO. 22K10
32 PC. SET
$9.25

NO. 22K11
53 PC. SET
$15.70

NO. 22K12
100 PC. SET
$32.00

"Jane Adams" Pattern

Bright gay flowers feature this decoration, with yellows and greens predominating. Dainty orchid buds also enhance the attractiveness of this lovely design. It is a two spray design. The handles are treated in appropriate colors.

This "Jane Adams" pattern is as attractive as a refreshing summer floral spray   sets off the modern dining table to such great advantage that knowin   ostesses are unusually enthusiastic about it. You, too, can be sure tha   hat it does for other tables it most assuredly can do for yours. The new   ctory" shape forms a perfect background for the smartness of its modern pattern. You will be interested in knowing that this shape was designed by a noted ceramic designer of the Cleveland Art School. This is truly a lovely shape

Victory shape dinnerware.

PEACH and CLOVER
Flair shape. Starter Set $9.95

MELODY LANE
Ranch Style shape. Starter set $6.95

SHAKER BROWN LIME
Flair shape. Starter set $9.95

old friends and new favorites

FRENCH PROVINCIAL
Flair shape. Starter set $9.95

PLANTATION
Ranch Style shape. Starter set $9.95

GERANIUM
Ranch Style shape. Starter set $5.95

WOODHUE
Flair shape. Starter set $8.95

the winning team for '52 by SALEM CHINA

Here's a partial showing of Salem's winning team for '52—established best-seller favorites and sparkling brand-new patterns created by famous designer Viktor Schreckengost in cooperation with market-wise merchandising specialists. Call in your Salem representative today...put this winning team to work for you! It's Salem China...a fifty year tradition of quality, reliability and advanced styling.

PRIMROSE
Ranch Style shape. Starter set $5.95

Look for this backstamp—the signet of Salem's master potters. It is your assurance of unfailing highest quality.

THE **SALEM CHINA** CO.
SALEM, OHIO
REPRESENTATIVES IN PRINCIPAL CITIES

Flair and Ranch shapes designed by Viktor Schreckengost for Salem China Co. from 1952 *Crockery and Glass Journal.*

the call is for
JACKSTRAW BLUE
on CONSTELLATION

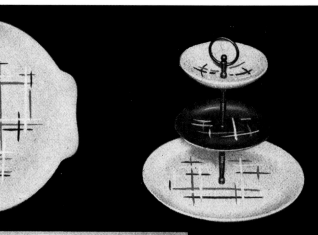

Constellation, appealing color contrast . . . off-white flecked with deep gray and the soft lustre of ebony . . . now made even more appealing with the addition of Salem's famous Jackstraw pattern . . . "Jackstraw Blue." Homemakers acclaimed the charming, modern Constellation shape . . . and they'll want it even more when they see Jackstraw Blue sparkling on it. Don't wait! Order from your Salem representative now!

Jackstraw Blue pattern on Constellation shape designed by Viktor Schreckengost for Salem China Co. from 1954 *Crockery and Glass Journal.*

Ben Seibel

Ben Seibel

Little biographical information could be found on Ben Seibel as to his education and place of birth. We do know that he died in the mid-1980s leaving a legacy of classic designs for collectors to gather and enjoy. He was a contemporary of such well-known designers as Eva Zeisel, Viktor Schreckengost and Russel Wright.

Ben Seibel designed the extremely successful line, Contempura, for the Steubenville China Company, Steubenville, Ohio. Due to Contempura's success for Steubenville, he was asked to do a line for Raymor made by the Roseville Pottery Company and called Raymor Modern Stoneware introduced in 1952. Raymor Modern Stoneware came in Avocado Green, Autumn Brown, Terra Cotta, Beach Grey and Contemporary White.

Brochure featuring Ben Seibel's Contempora dinnerware made by Steubenville China Co.

Here it is—the most exciting development in dinnerware since the advent of informal dining! Raymor Modern Stoneware combines cook-in, bake-in, serve-in features, with a delicacy of form, texture and color never before available in stoneware! And it's chip-resistant as well as oven-proof!

Brilliantly designed by Ben Seibel, Raymor Modern Stoneware offers a complete dinnerware service...encompassing distinctive new shapes especially created to fill contemporary dining needs. Accessory pieces, for example, include many multi-purpose units —such as casserole and bean pot services with trivets to keep heat off tables. For ease in handling, there are recessed grips on flatware and hollow-ware.

Sixteen-piece starter sets are retail priced at only $8.95 ($11.40 open stock). Starter sets and accessories are available in five colors—Autumn Brown, Avocado Green, Terra Cotta, Beach Grey and Contemporary White. Beautiful, functional, completely unique—here is dinnerware with exceptional sales potential for many seasons to come! Write for complete information.

Manufactured by **ROSEVILLE POTTERY, Inc.** Zanesville, Ohio
for Exclusive National Distribution by:
RICHARDS MORGENTHAU & CO.
225 Fifth Avenue, New York 10. N. Y.

Raymor coffee server.

Reprint featuring Ben Seibel's Raymor stoneware made by Roseville Pottery Inc. from 1952 *Crockery and Glass Journal.*

Raymor stoneware designed by Ben Seibel for Roseville Pottery Inc.

Raymor place setting.

Trade paper advertisement featuring Impromptu shape designed by Ben Seibel.

In 1956, the Iroquois China Company introduced the Ben Seibel designed Impromptu in Bridal White and seven original patterns. The original patterns were:

Stellar: delicate stars in gray, green and rust.

House of Flowers.

Pins and Beads: turquoise, taupe and brown.

Frolic: abstract forms in pink, rust, green, brown and charcoal.

Vision: gray points with blue accents.

Chrysanthemums: delicate blossoms with orange centers and brown petals.

Impromptu was offered in gift sets which was a very innovative marketing idea in 1956. Iroquois Impromptu was offered in the following pieces:

Impromptu pieces offered in 1956:

510	10" Dinner plate.
508	8" Salad plate.
507	6 1/2" Bread and butter.
580	Cup.
581	Saucer.
502	Fruit Compote.
503	Soup.
540	Cream.
541	Sugar/cover.
560	Open vegetable, 32 oz.
592	Small platter, 11".
593	Large platter, 13".
595	Salad bowl.
550	Coffee pot with cover.
582	Divided vegetable.
551	Water pitcher.
590	Gravy bowl.
591	Gravy stand.
587	Casserole with cover.
506	Relish tray.
594	Salt and pepper, pair.
570	Cruet with stopper.
571	Mustard with cover.
572	Condiment dish with brass.
573	Centerpiece dish.
574	Centerpiece insert.

PomPon pattern on Impromptu shape designed by Ben Seibel and made by Iroquois China Co. Row 1: Dinner plate, small platter, large platter. Row 2: Divided vegetable, covered sugar, sauce boat and liner, fruit compote, vegetable bowl, cup and saucer, relish tray, bread and butter plate, creamer.

A new shape, Informal was introduced in 1958. The key advertising word for Informal was "Cookmanship." Impromptu was flameproof but Informal had more capabilities as it could be used in the oven or on the stove and go right to the table.

The Informal line has "duplex" colors and is lined or faced with solid colors. The Informal line was launched with four patterns: Harvest Time, Lazy Daisy, Rosemary and Blue Diamonds. Harvest Time and Rosemary are shown.

Cooking items included a 10" covered fry pan, Dutch oven, one quart covered sauce pan, and 24 cup Samovar with stand.

Dinnerware items in Informal included:

710	Dinner plate.
708	Salad Breakfast plate.
780	Tea cup.
781	Tea saucer.
703	Lug soup.
740	Creamer.
741	Covered sugar.
723	Gumbo soup with cover.
760	Open vegetable.
792	Small platter, 12".
793	Large platter, 15".
787	Covered casserole, 2 quart.
782	Trivided Server.
794	Salt and pepper.
707	Butter/coaster/ashtray.
751	Coffee pot with cover.
770	Buffet Server insert.
770B	Revolving Base.

Informal did not prove to be as successful as Impromptu but even so, several other patterns were later added to the line. Perhaps the three year guarantee was more appealing than purchasing new china.

Inheritance was introduced in 1959 and was truly an elegant china. Not only was a new shape introduced with Inheritance, but new items that had traditionally been made of silver such as tea sets, vegetable bowls and salad bowls were offered as well.

Inheritance pieces offered in 1959:

910	Dinner plate.
908	Salad plate.
907	Bread and butter plate.
980	Tea cup.
981	Tea saucer.
990	Rim soup.
903	Cereal bowl.
902	Fruit bowl.
940	Creamer.
941	Sugar with cover.
960	Open vegetable.
992	Medium platter.
993	Large platter with wood stand.
995	Salad bowl with wood stand.
987	Casserole with cover and wood stand.
982	Divided vegetable with cover.
991	Gravy boat.
950	Tea pot with cover and wood stand.
901W	Lacquer serving tray.

Black lacquered stands enhanced the new Inheritance and were made to be used with the 1 1/2 quart casserole, salad bowl, platter, tea pot and tea set. There were no additional charges for the stands.

All the Iroquois Ben Seibel lines were offered in white, as was the Inheritance. Other Inheritance patterns included Baroque, Knollwood, Cotillion, Grecian Gold, Su-Shi, Medallion, Beige Rose, Dynasty Thane or Teuton, and Gold or Platinum Band. Additional patterns in Inheritance may yet come to light.

The last line Ben Seibel designed for Iroquois was Intaglio which again was available in plain white as well as patterns. The shapes were more subdued and this line was also guaranteed for three years against chipping and cracking. Some of the patterns for Intaglio were: Old English Pink, Old English Blue, Woodale, Blue Painted Daisy, Pink Painted Golden Dahlia, Blue Dahlia, Jade Rosette and Sun Rosette.

I continue to look for other patterns in any of the Iroquois lines, so if any of you discover, or think that you may have discovered one, please let me hear from you.

We know that Ben Seibel designed an Ovenproof Stoneware line for Haeger Pottery in Dundee, Illinois in 1971. He may have designed for other American companies as well. He was an integral part of the Mikasa operation and may have been with Mikasa at the time of his death.

Rosemary pattern on Informal shape designed by Ben Seibel and made by Iroquois China Co. Salad/breakfast plate, dinner plate, cup and saucer.

Harvest Time pattern on Informal shape designed by Ben Seibel and made by Iroquois China Co. Row 1: Salt and pepper, platter, creamer, two sizes of utility pitchers. Row 2: Divided vegetable, cup and saucer, salad plate, sugar bowl, vegetable bowl, bowl, dinner plate.

Brochure featuring Inheritance line designed by Ben Seibel.

OVENPROOF STONEWARE by Ben Seibel   **BURNT ORANGE SANDSTONE**

3206 Warmer
6″ x 3″

3210
7″ Casserole

3205
Covered
Casserole
10″ x 3½″

3212 Salad Bowl
10″ x 3½″

3213 Salad Bowl
7″ x 2½″

3208 Baking Dish
8½″ x 13″

3212

4241 Pitcher
Ht. 6½″

3207
Snack Tray 10″ x 7″

3209 Baking Dish
6½″ x 10″

3215 Pepper
Ht. 4″

3214 Salt

4240 Mug
11 oz.

3211 Covered Ramekin
Dia. 5″

Ben Seibel oven proof stoneware made for Haeger Potteries.

Three sizes of pitchers designed by J. Palin Thorley and made by Hall China Co.

J. Palin Thorley

Joseph Palin Thorley was born into a long line of English potters in Staffordshire, England, in 1892. Both sides of the family were potters. He was educated at the Hanley School of Art in Staffordshire, England. After art school, he served as an apprentice for Josiah Wedgwood and worked for other well known English potters before coming to the United States in 1929.

Shortly after he came to the United States he joined the Sebring Pottery Company in Sebring, Ohio, and designed their classic Leigh ware. He became art director of the American Chinaware Corporation which was a short-lived merger of eight or nine Ohio potteries. In great demand as a designer, he did design work for Taylor, Smith and Taylor, Hall China and others.

J. Palin Thorley moved to Williamsburg, Virginia in 1946, where he made reproduction 18th century ceramic pieces for the Colonial Williamsburg Foundation. His own studio pieces were produced in a garage workshop at his home.

Mr. Thorley's wife was ill during the late 1960s and early 1970s. It is said that, after his wife became ill, he never returned to his workshop. In fact, over ten years later his studio looked as if he had simply stepped away from the shop for a moment even though some newspapers used to cover wet pieces from the wheel or out of the mold were dated 1966. The shop had a sign that simply said "Ceramics." All of his Williamsburg, Virginia, pieces are signed Palin Thorley under an Aladdin shape lamp and Williamsburg, VA. Palin Thorley, genius, master ceramist, craftsman and artist, died in Williamsburg in 1986 at the age of 94.

Dorothy C. Thorpe

Dorothy Carpenter was born to George and Agatha Carpenter on January 5, 1901, in Salt Lake City, Utah. Little is known about her early life except that she loved piano music and studied music for many years. She attended the University of Utah. In 1923, she married George A. Thorpe of Los Angeles, California.

Dorothy Thorpe's career in glass had an unusual beginning. Her husband, George, had suffered reversals during the depression. Mrs. Thorpe's chance finding of a broken wine bottle in the street was the beginning of her very successful career and ultimately led to her own glass designing and sandblasting company.

Mrs. Thorpe took the broken bottle home thinking she could make something out of it. She made a groove below the neck and broke off the top part. She then took the bottle to a glass factory and had the rough edges ground down. She took the bottle home and covered the wine bottle with masking tape, cutting away part of the tape to expose her initials. After returning the bottle to the glass factory for sandblasting, she removed the tape, leaving her initials sharply incised on the wine bottle turned tumbler. She then decorated the tumbler with raffia.

The very next day Dorothy visited a Los Angeles department store which placed a big order for her highball glasses. Instead of going to work the next day, her husband went to all of the city dumps and gathered bottles. The Thorpes did not have a telephone so their neighbors would let them know when an order had been phoned in.

From these humble depression era beginnings, Dorothy Thorpe's originals were sold all over the world. By 1947, she had her own manufacturing plant. A prolific designer, she is credited with having 2,000 glass designs manufactured. She also designed tablecloths and other table accessories. In her earlier years, she won more than 100 awards for her needlework.

While Dorothy Thorpe is better known for her glass designing, she also designed a few dinnerware lines. Expect Dorothy Thorpe designs to become more important in the collecting world.

Dorothy C. Thorpe died at Carlsbad, California, on August 4, 1989.

Floribunda pattern glassware designed by Dorothy C. Thorpe from *China, Glass & Tableware*, 1965. *Reprinted with permission of Doctorow Communications, Inc., Clifton, N.J.*

Dorothy C. Thorpe

16" Sandwich Plate ($10.00 retail)
Shown are part of a 3 dimensional, handmade, sand carved, group of hostess accessories in the FLORIBUNDA pattern. These delightful originals retail from $2.50 to $20.00.

Dinnerware designed by Dorothy C. Thorpe (pattern unknown).

Persimmon pattern designed by Dorothy C. Thorpe, made in Japan in
1960s. The persimmon color is very unusual; the decoration is in gold, and
the insides of the cups are lined in gold. Row 1: Salad or dessert plate,
dinner plate. Row 2: Coffee server, cup and saucer.

RUSSEL WRIGHT

Russel Wright

Lebanon, Ohio, was the birthplace of Russel Wright in 1904. Mr. Wright attended Cincinnati Academy of Art in Columbus, Ohio, and the Princeton School of Architecture.

Over a thirty year span he designed many products and furnishings. Lamps, flatware, furniture, aluminum, linens, chrome, plastic dinnerware, and dinnerware were just some of the products he designed. It is his dinnerware designs that we are interested in here.

American Modern

Russel Wright's first important dinnerware line was American Modern made by the Steubenville Pottery Company, Steubenville, Ohio. American Modern was introduced in 1939 with no decoration on innovative shapes with unusual colors. The six original colors were Seafoam Blue, Coral, Chartreuse, Grey, White and Bean Brown. Cedar Green, Cantaloupe, Glacier Blue, and Black Chutney were added sometime later. General run pieces in American Modern are still available but some pieces and colors are difficult to find. American Modern met the changing needs of the American homemaker. Home entertaining was becoming more popular and there was a need for more casual and affordable dinnerware. Russel Wright packaged American Modern in four place settings at inexpensive prices that were especially appealing to newly married couples.

American Modern, as an earthenware, breaks and chips easily; even so, it became an American classic that outsold any dinnerware line ever made except the Virginia Rose shape including all of its many variations.

American Modern pattern designed by Russel Wright and made by Steubenville Pottery Co. Vegetable bowl, serving plate, small bowl, creamer, cup, plate, gravy boat, and liner.

Iroquois Casual

The problems with American Modern were apparent to Russel Wright. His next dinnerware line was Casual and made by Iroquois. Casual was a high-fired china and guaranteed not to break or chip in normal use. Introductory colors of Casual were Sugar White, Ice Blue and Lemon Yellow. Other colors were added later: Nutmeg, Charcoal, Ripe Apricot, and Pink Sherbet.

The first Iroquois Casual was the "pinch" shape. Iroquois was restyled by Russel Wright. Iroquois Casual became lighter and had a smooth appearance.

Cookware was added to the Iroquois Casual line but is difficult to find.

Color advertisement featuring later addition of new colors to Iroquois Casual China: Nutmeg Brown, Lettuce Green, Ripe Apricot, Lemon, Charcoal, and Pink Sherbet.

Iroquois Casual China in rare color (Iroquois Aqua). Salt and pepper, creamer, sugar, cup and saucer, dinner plate, covered butter dish.

Iroquois Aqua teapot.

Iroquois Brick Red sugar, creamer, cup and saucer, covered butter dish.

Highlight-Paden City Pottery

Highlight was made by the Paden City Pottery Company and marketed by the Justin Tharaud Company. Highlight is very difficult to find. It was advertised in open stock in Black Pepper, Blueberry, Nutmeg, and Snow Glaze.

Highlight pattern designed by Russel Wright for Paden City Pottery Co. Shown is Blueberry plate, two sizes bowls, cup and saucer.

Sterling-Russel Wright Ware

In 1949, Russel Wright designed a restaurant-hotel line for the Sterling China Company in green, yellow, gray, brown and white. Sterling China designed by Russel Wright was short-lived, difficult to find and often not marked. Collectors of Russel Wright designs can readily identify the distinguished Russel Wright shapes.

Sterling Russel Wright Ware restaurant/hotel ware. Shown is an Ivy Green Sterling coffee bottle, demi cup and saucer.

Golden Spice

General Electric clock designed by Russell Wright for Harker Pottery.

White Clover-Harker Pottery Company

White Clover was a slight departure for Russel Wright. It was a combination of subdued shapes and Harker's engobe process. White Clover was introduced in the early fifties in Golden Spice, Meadow Green, Charcoal and Coral Sand. A clock face was also made by Harker.

Knowles Esquire

Esquire was introduced in the mid-fifties when many pottery companies were ailing or had already succumbed to the pressures of foreign imports, plastics and wage disputes. Not an extensive line, Esquire did not prove to be popular. In relation to the popular American Modern and Iroquois Casual, Esquire was short-lived.

When Russel Wright collectors are fortunate enough to find a large piece of Esquire, the pattern name will be included in the backstamp. Patterns are: Botanica on beige background, Grass on blue background, Queen Anne's Lace on white background, Snowflower on pink background and Solar on White. There were also three solid colored lines with no decoration in Knowles Esquire.

If Russel Wright designs are your "dish," you must get *The Collectors Encyclopedia of Russel Wright* by Ann Kerr, available from Collectors Books, Paducah, Kentucky. Mrs. Kerr is "the" expert on Russel Wright and is also my dearest friend. Thanks, Ann!

Grass pattern on Esquire line designed by Russel Wright for Knowles China Co.

Eva Zeisel

Eva Zeisel

It was my honor and privilege to be a guest in the home of Eva Zeisel a few years ago. Mrs. Zeisel was a charming and gracious hostess, even though she was in the midst of preparing her retrospective at the time. It was later shown in Montreal and was to become part of the Smithsonian Institution Traveling Exhibition Services. The Eva Zeisel Retrospective was shown in 1983 at the Brooklyn Museum, the Art Institute of Chicago, New Jersey State Museum, Everson Museum of Art, Saint Louis Art Museum, and the Flint Institute of Art, Flint, Michigan. It was also shown in several other countries including Holland.

Eva Zeisel was born in 1906 in Budapest, Hungary, to Alexander Stricker and Laura Polanyi. Her father was a well-to-do factory owner and her mother held a doctorate degree in history. She painted when she was very young and after a short stay at the Royal Academy of Fine Arts, she decided to become a potter. She served her apprenticeship to a local potter and was given jobs that any male counterpart would have been given. But more importantly for us, Eva learned to throw and glaze pottery.

Her early travels and experiences are most fascinating. If you are interested in an in-depth treatise on Eva Zeisel's life, I suggest that you read *Eva Zeisel, Designer for Industry*, distributed by The Brooklyn Museum, 200 Eastern Parkway, Brooklyn, New York 11238. Also, there is an interesting article that appeared in the *New Yorker* magazine, April 10, 1987, entitled "Profiles, the Present Moment" by Susannah Lessard.

Eva came to this country in 1938 with her husband, Hans Zeisel. She was recommended to Simon Slobodkin, a factory representative, who ordered a line of giftware. She was soon asked to do another line of giftware for the Bayridge Company in Trenton and this line was called American Art China - Eva Zeisel.

Eva began teaching at Pratt Institute in 1939. While at Pratt, she was asked to design a dinnerware line for Sears & Roebuck. This line was Stratoware by Sears (see illustration). Stratoware was only produced for about a year. In the 1942 Sears catalog, only the Industrial Design Department of Pratt Institute was given credit. By 1943, Eva Zeisel and her associates were credited in the catalog.

Eva Zeisel's association with Castleton China Company in 1942 was truly the beginning of her exceptional career. At the recommendation of the Museum of Modern Art, she designed the Museum line for Castleton which was developed between 1942 and 1945 and introduced in a one-woman show at the Museum of Modern Art in 1946. Museum has clean, classic white lines with decorations added at a later date. The Museum line was advertised as "the first translucent china dinnerware produced in the United States." The project was suggested to Louis Hellman, president of the Castleton China Company, by the director of the department of industrial design at the museum, Eliot Noyes. He also suggested that Eva be the designer. The museum line was exhibited at the Museum of Modern Art, New York.

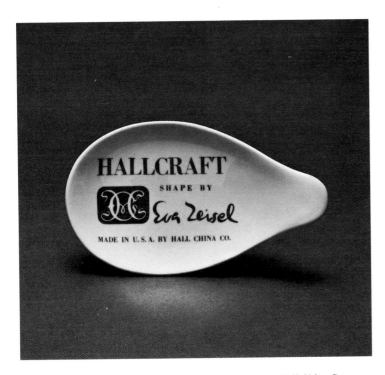

Hallcraft advertising piece designed by Eva Zeisel for Hall China Co.

Pieces designed by Eva Zeisel, 1939-1940, for Bay Ridge, Co. *Photograph courtesy of Eva Zeisel.*

Her next American undertaking was to design in 1946 the ever elusive Town and Country line for Red Wing Pottery, Red Wing, Minnesota. Town and Country was ready and presented in 1947. Town and Country comes in five colors. The salt and pepper shakers were designed prior to the Schmoo character. In our conversations, Eva was adamant that the Town and Country shakers not be referred to as "Schmoo". Town and Country is now a desirable and hard to find dinnerware line.

Eva's next American line was one for the Riverside Ceramic Company. The only piece of Riverside I have ever seen was in Eva's home. Riverside was unique in that for the first time, she only designed the shapes and was not involved in the glazing process, as had previously been the case. The lovely Riverside pieces have successfully eluded me.

Eva Zeisel's most commercially successful dinnerware line was produced by the Hall China Company in the 1950s. It was marketed by a sales organization, Midhurst China Company, under the Hallcraft label. The first shape, Classic, or Tomorrow's Classic began to be produced by Hall around 1952. Classic was available in white. Some hollowware was available in satin black. Many decorations adorned the Classic shape.

Eva told me that her friend and assistant, Irene Haas, designed Frost Flowers. Mrs. Zeisel herself suggested to Eric Blegvad that the grill work at her New York city apartment would make an interesting design. Thus, the decoration, Buckingham, came to be. Abstract artist, Charles Seliger, and others also supplied decorations for the Classic shape.

Museum shape designed by Eva Zeisel for Castleton China Co. Reprinted from *Everyday Art Quarterly, A Guide to Well Designed Products,* Fall 1946. Walker Art Center, Minneapolis, MN.

EVA ZEISEL is the designer of the first translucent china dinnerware, *modern in shape,* that has been produced in the United States. It is the result of successful co-operation between the designer, the manufacturer (Castleton China) and the Museum of Modern Art.

The exceptional quality of the material permitted thin edges that emphasize its clear translucency; bases of cups and bowls are heavier for greater stability.

The china, ivory white in color, depends on refinement of shape and flawless surface quality for its beauty. Most pieces are round; but variations have been introduced in some bowls and platters whose rims are flowing and modulated.

Shown only in a few New York stores to date, the china will be available nationally in 1947. A complete dinner service is being produced: bowls, vegetable dishes, chop tray, covered casserole, gravy boat and ladle, salts and peppers, tea pot, coffee pot, sugar and creamers—in addition to several sizes of plates and cups.

Stratoware pattern designed by Eva Zeisel for Sears & Roebuck. Reprinted from *Sears Catalog*, 1942.

In 1964, Eva Zeisel's "Z" dinnerware line was produced by Hyalyn. The few pieces that I have seen have a spectacular high glaze. Information about the Hyalyn line is skimpy and it is believed to have been a small line of decorative objects as opposed to a dinnerware line. To the best of my knowledge, Hyalyn was the last work Eva Zeisel did for any American companies.

1933	Eva Zeisel comes to United States
1938	Designs giftware line
1939	Begins teaching at Pratt Institute
1940	Begins association with Castleton China Company
1940-42	Designs Stratoware for Sears
1942-45	Museum line, made by Castleton with cooperation of the Museum of Modern Art (Ivory glaze-limited distribution)
1946	Designed Town and Country for Red Wing Pottery
1947	Museum line available nationally; Red Wing produced Town and Country; Riverside Ceramic Company
1949	Norleans Meito China made in Japan; Museum appears with Mandalay decoration
1950	Tomorrows Classic-Classic Shape manufactured by Hall-marketed by Midhurst China Company under Hallcraft name
1952-53	Zeiselware produced by Western Stoneware, Monmouth, Illinois
1954	Designed Seal brown cookware and kitchen accessories for the Hall China Company
1956-57	Century shape, made by Hall also marketed by Midhurst under Hallcraft name
1964	"Z" ware, made by Hyalyn, small cookware line

Town and Country designed by Eva Zeisel for Red Wing Pottery Co. Red Wing colors were Dusk Blue, Forest Green, Metallic Brown, Chartreuse, Gray, Rust, Sand, and Peach. Pictured are two sizes bowls, salt and pepper, coaster, creamer and sugar, covered soup, gravy boat and attached liner (Red Wing's Concord shape, No. C22, with metallic glaze). Salt and pepper shakers are Town and Country shapes but are Red Wing colors.

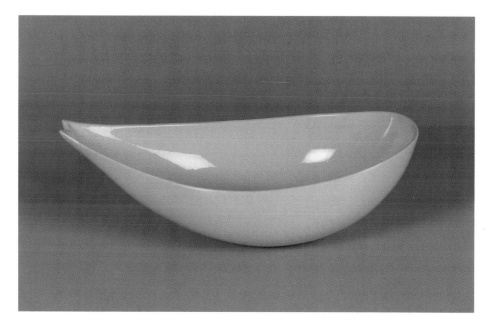

Bowl designed by Eva Zeisel for Riverside China Co. (Also referred to Riverside Ceramic Co.) *From the collection of Charles Alexander.*

Opposite Page:
Norleans China designed by Eva Zeisel made in Japan. Reprinted from *China, Glass & Accessories*, 1949.

Advertisement for Riverside Ceramic Co.

Riverside Ceramic Co. jug and tumbler.

MANDALAY by Ching-Chih Yee, first design to be created for Castleton's "Museum" shape, designed by Eva Zeisel; pattern is featured in current exhibit of Castleton Collection now on tour. Castleton China, Inc., 212 Fifth Avenue, New York.

Mandalay design added to Museum shape in 1949.

CASTLETON CHINA

CASTLETON once again assumes its leadership in ceramic design by creating the first dinner service of free form shapes in fine china with patterns keyed to the modern mood.

Lyana decoration added to Museum shape in 1950.

NATIONALLY ADVERTISED

CASTLETON CHINA, INC. • 212 FIFTH AVE., NEW YORK

Eva Zeisel shown working with Buckingham design on Classic shape.
Photograph courtesy of Eva Zeisel.

Arizona decoration designed by Charles Seliger on Eva Zeisel's classic shape. *Photograph courtesy of Eva Zeisel.*

◆ The Hall China Co.

Smart, new, 20-piece line of fireproof cooking and kitchen accessories features new matte Seal Brown-colored bodies dramatically contrasted with stark white linings and lids. A modern, abstract design in shades of brown, mauve, and blue is used to decorate the lids. Included in the line is a 6-cup teapot; spice or condiment jar; French, 2-handled casserole (2-quart capacity); oval, covered casserole (½-quart capacity); and an individual casserole or left over dish. Items will range in price from $2 to $6.95 each retail. Factory is located in E. Liverpool, Ohio.

Seal brown coffee set has white lining, lids. Pot, $2.75; sugar, creamer, $1.50 ea. Hall China, E. Liverpool, O.

Seal Brown cooking and kitchen accessories designed by Eva Zeisel.

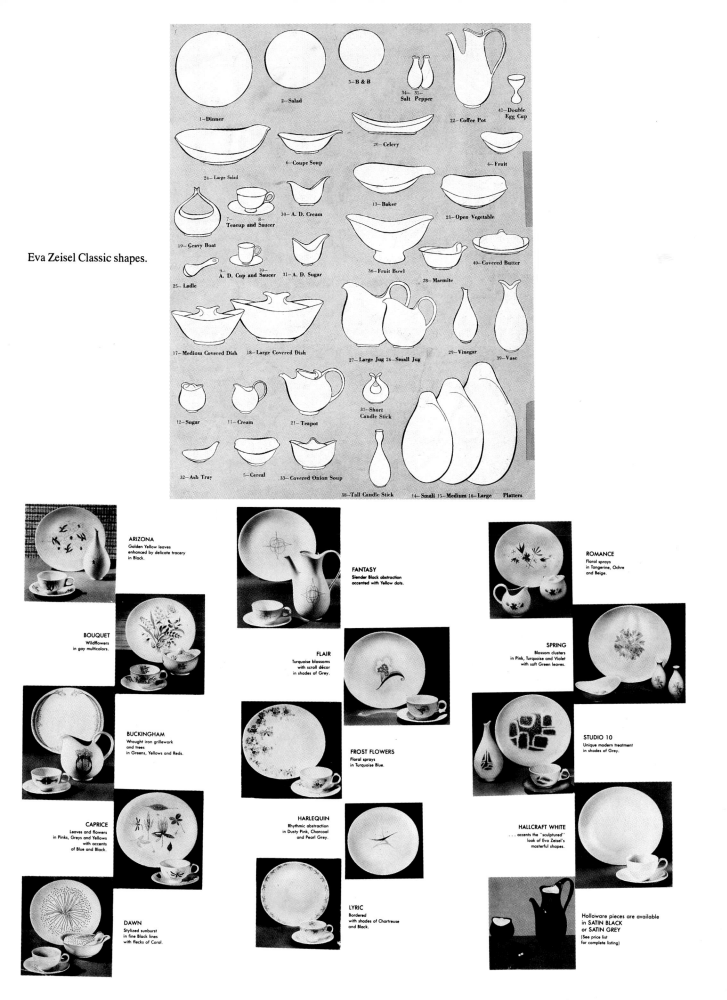

Eva Zeisel Classic shapes.

1—Dinner
2—Salad
3—B & B
34— 35—Salt Pepper
22— Coffee Pot
41—Double Egg Cup
20—Celery
6—Coupe Soup
4— Fruit
24— Large Salad
30—A. D. Cream
13— Baker
23— Open Vegetable
7— 8—Teacup and Saucer
19—Gravy Boat
9— 10—A. D. Cup and Saucer
31—A. D. Sugar
36—Fruit Bowl
40— Covered Butter
25—Ladle
28— Marmite
17—Medium Covered Dish
18— Large Covered Dish
27— Large Jug 26—Small Jug
29— Vinegar
39—Vase
12—Sugar
11— Cream
21— Teapot
37—Short Candle Stick
38—Tall Candle Stick
32—Ash Tray
5—Cereal
33— Covered Onion Soup
14— Small 15—Medium 16—Large Platters

ARIZONA
Golden Yellow leaves
enhanced by delicate tracery
in Black.

FANTASY
Slender Black abstraction
accented with Yellow dots.

ROMANCE
Floral sprays
in Tangerine, Ochre
and Beige.

BOUQUET
Wildflowers
in gay multicolors.

FLAIR
Turquoise blossoms
with scroll décor
in shades of Grey.

SPRING
Blossom clusters
in Pink, Turquoise and Violet
with soft Green leaves.

BUCKINGHAM
Wrought iron grillework
and trees
in Greens, Yellows and Reds.

FROST FLOWERS
Floral sprays
in Turquoise Blue.

STUDIO 10
Unique modern treatment
in shades of Grey.

CAPRICE
Leaves and flowers
in Pinks, Greys and Yellows
with accents
of Blue and Black.

HARLEQUIN
Rhythmic abstraction
in Dusty Pink, Charcoal
and Pearl Grey.

HALLCRAFT WHITE
. . . accents the "sculptured"
look of Eva Zeisel's
masterful shapes.

DAWN
Stylized sunburst
in fine Black lines
with flecks of Coral.

LYRIC
Bordered
with shades of Chartreuse
and Black.

Holloware pieces are available
in SATIN BLACK
or SATIN GREY
(See price list
for complete listing)

Various patterns on Eva Zeisel's Classic shapes.

The Century shape was produced about 1956 or 1957. The pitchers and teapots seem to be more subdued than Classic but the plates have an unusual tear-drop shape. Century was also available in plain white with a variety of decorations and was also made by the Hall China Company.

Century shape pieces designed by Eva Zeisel for Hall China.

Century shape plate designed by Eva Zeisel.

Zeisel Ware designed by Eva Zeisel for Western Stoneware.

Covered stoneware jar set designed by Eva Zeisel for Western Stoneware.

Zeisel Ware teapot designed by Eva Zeisel for Western Stoneware.

Eva Zeisel Western stoneware backstamp.

Eva Zeisel stoneware.

Z Ware designed by Eva Zeisel for Hyalyn Porcelain.

Below: Hyalyn Porcelain produces these handsome porcelain pieces: ice bucket (l.) and casserole. The designer is Eva Zeisel.

Advertisement for Z Ware designed by Eva Zeisel for Hyalyn Porcelain,
China, Glass & Tableware, April 1964. *Reprinted with permission of
Doctorow Communications, Inc., Clifton, N.J.*

Drip Glazes

Vonlynn

Drip glazes on dinnerware are "subtle blendings" and graduations of colors that make for a casual appearance. While the drip-glazed ware appears casual to the collector, much care and preparation go into the making of such ware.

The flow of the glaze had to be controlled to achieve the proper artistic effect. One method of controlling the drip of the glaze was achieved by applying the glaze in such thin layers that there was not a lot of weight to speed the flow of the glazes. Duration and temperature during firing were also important factors in controlling the flow.

An excellent example of pleasing drip-glazed ware is the Vonlynn's of Hollywood. Vonlynn's was incorporated from 1946 to 1950. The pieces shown are identified as Vonlynn's in a 1947 *Crockery and Glass Journal*. However, one of the pieces in the photograph is marked Allan of California. Allan of California was incorporated in 1946 and the incorporation status dissolved in 1947.

Fictitious names are not listed with the state of California but it is my conclusion that Allan was a name used by Vonlynn. At any rate, we will refer to it as Vonlynn and it is a pleasing example of drip-glazed ware.

Winart did make some interesting pieces for the patio and pieces for casual dining. For complete information on Winart Potteries and Tamac Pottery, see *Frankoma and Other Oklahoma Potteries* by Tom and Phyllis Bess, published by Schiffer Publishing Company.

Row 1: Vonlynn's of California bowl, cup and saucer, different style cup and saucer, pitcher, tumbler. Row 2: Bowl, plate, cream soup and liner, vegetable bowl.

Tamac

Tamac was made in Perry, Oklahoma, from the mid-forties until the seventies. Tamac has recently found favor with collectors and prices are climbing rapidly.

Not a true drip glaze like Vonlynn and Winart, Tamac is more recognizable by its distinctive shapes and colors. Tamac was made in Frosty Pine, Frosty Fudge (both shown), Raspberry, and Avocado.

Row 1: Tamac plate, snack plate, small plate. Row 2: Mug, ashtray, cup and saucer, pitcher, salt and pepper, tumbler, bowl and saucer, creamer, two sizes bowls.

Winart

Another example of colorful combination of colors and drip glazes is the ware made by Winart of Oklahoma. Some of the Winart color combinations are very pleasing and some, quite frankly, are not so pleasing.

Winart did make some interesting pieces for the patio and pieces for casual dining. For complete information on Winart Potteries and Tamac Pottery, see *Frankoma and Other Oklahoma Potteries* by Tom and Phyllis Bess, published by Schiffer Publishing Company.

Row 1: Winart Drip Glaze ware pitcher, coffee mug, oversize pitcher, pitcher. Row 2: Plate, covered bowl, plate.

Blue with frost creamer with original Winart Pottery sticker.

Winart barbecue serving set in wrought iron frame (Bowl missing in bottom of wrought iron frame).

Coffee mugs showing variety of Winart colors.

Chapter Seven: The Best of The Unknowns

There are always a few miscellaneous items that do not seem to fit any particular place but are important enough to be included.

This set of dishes with pine cone design has such unusual shapes that it had to be included. It is possible that they were made in Colorado but none are marked and I have no further information.

A yellow glazed mug with an unusual handle and base appears to be from the 1920s. I had never seen this mug before finding a dozen in an antique shop. The glaze reminds me of Sebring but again, no mark, no clue.

The Calla lily plate was made in the San Jose Mission Pottery in San Antonio, Texas. I have received last minute information on the pottery and we will learn more about this one. If you have information concerning any of these items, please let me hear from you.

This hand-decorated plate is from the American Way, Russel Wright's merchandising co-op, but the maker is unknown.

Wallace China Co. Storz advertising plates designed by Till Goodan.
Most of Western Ware pieces are from the collection of Johnny and Bonnie McCroskey.

Westward Ho

While Westward Ho may not be the best in Western ware, it certainly is the hottest with collectors. Westward Ho was designed by Till Goodan and manufactured by The Wallace China Company of Los Angeles. It was distributed by W.C. Wentz, a crackerjack jobber and sales organization.

All three lines are on a "saddle-tan" background with the designs themselves being mostly dark and rusty brown. All designs are under the glaze. According to a 1948 trade publication, all three patterns were made in the following pieces:

WH100 Dinner plate - Size 10 3/4."
WH101 Cup and Saucer - 10 ounces.
WH102 Oval platter - 15 1/2".
WH103 Oval vegetable dish - 12".
WH104 Round vegetable dish - 8".
WH105 Large salt and pepper shakers - 5 1/4".
WH106 Salad bowl-13" diameter, depth 5".
WH107 Individual soup or salad bowl - 5 3/4".
WH108 Chop plate - 13".
WH109 Bread and Butter plate - 7".
WH110 Sugar bowl or Ramekin - 4 1/2".
WH111 Cream pitcher.
WH112 Cup and Saucer - 7 1/2 ounces.
WH114 Luncheon plate - 9".

The authentic Westward Ho line by Wallace should be found marked with either or both marks (shown). Although it is of restaurant weight, Westward Ho was designed for the retail trade, particularly for outdoor barbecues.

Westward Ho

WH200 dinner plate, 10¾".
9.00 doz.
WH201 cup and
saucer
10 oz.   6.90 doz.
WH202 oval platter...
15½" ...20.40 doz.
W203 oval baker . . .
12" .....16.00 doz.
WH205 large S and P
shakers 9.00 doz. pr.
WH207 salad or soup
bowl, 5¾" 4.80 doz.

Heavy Barbeque Ware in
Adobe Brown or Mission Blue.

m.c. Wentz Co.   BRACK SHOPS BUILDING
527 W. SEVENTH ST., LOS ANGELES 14

SEPTEMBER, 1945 ★ CHINA AND GLASS ★ Page 29

"Rodeo forms motif for barbecue ware by Western artist" was the lead-in for a 1945 article about Till Goodan in a trade publication featuring the Westward Ho line of Western ware.

According to a 1948 trade publication, three different patterns made up the Westward Ho dinnerware line. The three patterns shown were Pioneer Trails, Rodeo, and Boots and Saddles. Pioneer Trails depicts covered wagon train borders on all pieces with center designs depicting the early history of the pioneer west. Rodeo pattern has ranch brand borders with center designs depicting different rodeo events such as roping and rodeo riding. Boots and Saddles also has ranch brand borders with boot and saddle center designs.

Did you know that Westward Ho was also made in Adobe Brown or Mission Blue and again was referred to as "Barbecue Ware"? This information comes from a 1945 trade publication. The numbers are WH200 series as opposed to the Western decorated pieces.

Westward Ho barbecue ware in Adobe Brown or Mission Blue from a 1945 trade publication.

Row 1: Steer Head divided plate (maker unknown), novelty dinner bell (maker unknown), Chuck Wagon plate (maker unknown). Row 2: Spice set, made in Japan for Fred Rogers Co., San Francisco, novelty napkin holder.

Row 1: Syracuse China plate, cup, dinner plate. Plates are Syracuse Econo-Rim. Row 2: Syracuse China Indian plate, branding iron plate, cup and saucer.

Row 1: Wallace Rodeo shaker, novelty wooden salt and pepper shakers, dinner bell, toothpick holder, Wallace Rodeo demi cup. Row 2: Napkin corral, steak pick, novelty picks.

Row 1: Wallace Chuck Wagon cup and saucer, Wallace Pioneer Trails chop plate, Pioneer Trails small plate. Row 2: Wallace Chuck Wagon bread plate, dinner plate, creamer, individual syrup or creamer.

Wellsville China Co. Arizona Stockyards plate.

Row 1: Syracuse China Co. "Cowboy Boots" two small plates, Mayer China Co. "Wagon" dinner plate, cup and saucer, small plate. Row 2: Shenango China platter, novelty toothpick (made in Japan), Tepco Western Traveler divided plate.

Row 1: Homer Laughlin steak platter. Row 2: Holman Co. Cattle Brand novelty salt and pepper, Shenango China "Roper" plate.

Wallace syrup pitcher and plate.

Variety of Western motif pieces.

Row 1: Vernon Winchester '73 dessert plate, creamer and sugar, dinner plate. Row 2: Cup and saucer, salt and pepper, 6" plate, bowl, divided vegetable.

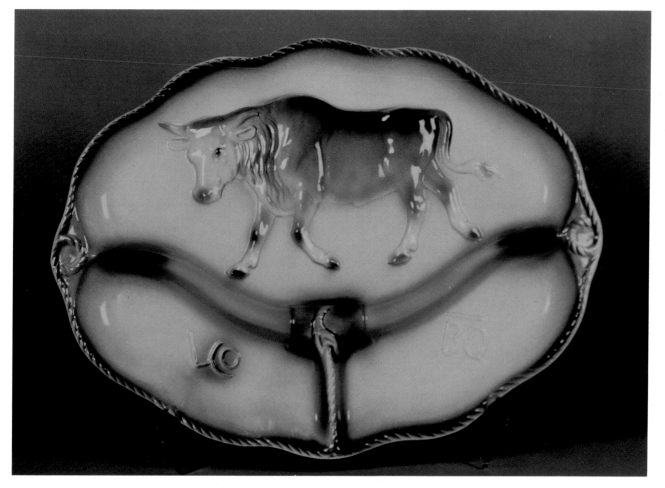

Extra large barbecue platter made by Lane of California.

Row 1: Jackson China cup and saucer, platter, mug. Row 2: Wallace cup
and saucer, El Rancho plate, Rod's Steak House small pitcher.

Row 1: Wallace ashtray, Westward Ho Boots and Saddles dinner plate,
bread or dessert plate. Row 2: Wallace two small plates, mug and Storz
advertising plate.

Wallace China Davey Crockett mug.

"Tepco"

The "Tepco" (The Technical Porcelain and Chinaware) Company was located in El Cerrito, California. "Tepco" was established in 1918 and in the 1960s was considered the largest manufacturer of hotel and restaurant chinaware west of the Mississippi.

All of "Tepco's" decorations and line treatments are under the glaze. The "Tepco" chinaware product then underwent a two-fire process leaving a hard glaze that was detergent resistant and would not rub off.

Shown is a poor copy of "Tepco" Branding Iron pattern restaurant ware and Western Traveler. Several different pieces were available in both patterns.

"Tepco" ware was available only through jobbers.

𝒯HE DAYS of the Pony Express are passed and perhaps forgotten, but "Tepco China" tried to bring back a memory of the old West, in the pattern called "Western Traveler."

In a way, like the Pony Express, "Tepco" has contributed to the development of the West. The present company was established in 1918 and today, is one of the largest manufacturers of 100 percent Vitrified Hotel and Restaurant Chinaware west of the Mississippi River.

Good china makers are not to be found in the labor market — they must be made. There are men that have been with the Tepco organization for thirty years. These men teach to the young employees all their knowledge and experience that they themselves have accumulated.

These employees take pride in their work, and are enthusiastic to produce a product that is foremost in their field. Their efforts give you added quality, greater durability, and superior appearance.

Besides the "Western Traveler" pattern "Tepco China" can be had in a great many other decorations or line treatments. Any combination of colors can be had to suit any color scheme in print, decal or colored band and line treatments, with or without special crest or monogram. Also Plain White or Plain Sunglow Ware.

All decorations and line treatments are put on under the glaze and will not wear off in any washing compound, soap suds, or sulphuric acid. Each dish undergoes a two fire process, which leaves a high, hard glaze.

We are exceedingly proud of the Tepco factory and wish to extend to you an invitation to visit us and let us show you our modern up-to-date process, which we believe helps to make "Tepco" the finest chinaware on the market today.

Technical Porcelain and China Ware Co.

Technical Porcelain and China Ware Company

Western Traveler pattern from 1950s Tepco catalog. Several different pieces were available in both patterns.

Technical Porcelain and China Ware Company

This picture belongs to: 2 906 040

PRICE LIST

TECHNICAL PORCELAIN & CHINAWARE COMPANY

Home of "TEPCO" and "PAMCO" Vitrified Chinaware

6416 Manila Street LAndscape 5-0960 El Cerrito, Calif.

WESTERN TRAVELER — BRANDING IRON

Standard or Narrow Rim

Actual Size	Trade Size	Article	Selling Price
		BAKERS	
5¼ in.	2½ in.	Rolled Edge	$ 8.24
5¾ in.	3 in.	Rolled Edge	8.44
10 in.	8 in.	Rolled Edge	21.14
12 in.	10 in.	Rolled Edge	30.80
		BOULLIONS	
7 oz.		St. Francis, Unhandled	7.86
		BOWLS	
5¾ in.	30s	Special Low Foot, Thick	11.90
5½ in.	30s	Low Foot, Thick	11.90
5 in.	36s	Low Foot, Thick	10.84
4¼ in.	42s	Low Foot, Thick	9.36
4 in.	48s	Low Foot, Thick	8.72
5⅞ in.	36s	Oatmeals, Rolled Edge	7.66
6¼ in.	30s	Oatmeals, Rolled Edge	9.36
10 in.		Soup Bowls	39.56
4¼ in.		Chinese Rice Bowls	10.84
3 in.		Chinese Tea Cups	7.54
6⅜ in.		Chop Suey Bowls, Low Foot	19.32
5¾ in.		Chop Suey Comport	17.32
		BUTTERS	
	2½ in.	Double Thick	3.44
		CELERY TRAYS	
7½ in.			19.32
9¾ in.			28.34
		COFFEE CUPS—HANDLED	
	7½ oz.	Boston Teas, Block Hld.	9.56
	7½ oz.	California, Welded Hld.	9.56
	6 oz.	Texas	9.56
	6½ oz.	Cascade	10.32
	8 oz.	Phild.	9.56
	10 oz.	Saxon	10.32
	6½ oz.	Ship	10.32
	6½ oz.	Texas Ship	10.32
	7½ oz.	Atlantic	9.56
	3¾ oz.	Saxon—A.D.—Demi-Tasse	7.24
	6½ oz.	Wilbur	9.56
		COFFEE CUPS—UNHANDLED	
	8 oz.	Phild.	8.20
	10 oz.	Saxon	8.20
	13 oz.	Saxon Q.M.C.	9.14
		EGG CUPS	
		Wheat Egg	8.72
		Double Wheat Egg	9.35

Actual Size	Trade Size	Article	Selling Price
		COFFEE SAUCERS	
	5 in.	Wilbur	$ 5.96
	5¾ in.	Rolled Edge, Cascade	5.96
	6¼ in.	Rolled Edge, Wide Foot	5.96
	6 in.	Rolled Edge, Narrow Foot	5.96
	4¾ in.	A. D. Demi-Tasse	5.48
	5½ in.	Ship	5.96
		COMPORTS	
5 in.		Rolled Edge	27.92
7 in.		Rolled Edge	30.98
		CREAMERS	
	¾ oz.	Tankard	6.40
	1 oz.	Tankard	6.40
	2 oz.	Tankard	7.06
	3 oz.	Tankard	7.72
	4 oz.	Duquesne, Handled	10.42
	7 oz.	Duquesne, Handled	11.90
		FRUITS	
4½ in.	3 in.	Rolled Edge	5.06
4⅝ in.	3½ in.	Double Thick, Flat	5.48
4¾ in.	3½ in.	Rolled Edge	5.48
5⅛ in.	4 in.	Rolled Edge	5.70
5 in.	5 in.	Vernon	5.70
		GRAPEFRUITS	
5¾ in.		#1 Rolled Edge, Small	8.50
6½ in.		#2 Rolled edge, Large	9.36
		MUGS	
	5 oz.	Tom & Jerry	
	5 oz.	Pirate Handled	
	8 oz.	Lawrence, Handled	12.96
	6 oz.	Early California, Handled	12.96
	8 oz.	Lawrence, Unhandled	8.20
	12 oz.	Root Beer	21.44
	6½ oz.	Ritz. Handled	12.96
	7 oz.	Hot Chocolate	
		NAPPIES	
	3 in.	Rolled Edge	9.36
	4 in.	Rolled Edge	10.84
		MUSTARDS	
	4 oz.	Vienna, Unhld. Covered	12.74
	6½ oz.	Vienna, Unhld. Covered	14.02

Actual Size	Trade Size	Article	Selling Price
		PLATES	
5½ in.	3 in.	Rolled Edge	$ 5.48
6¼ in.	4 in.	Rolled Edge	6.60
6⅞ in.	4½ in.	Rolled Edge	7.44
7¼ in.	5 in.	Rolled Edge	8.08
8⅛ in.	6 in.	Rolled Edge	10.00
9 in.	7 in.	Rolled Edge	11.90
9¾ in.	8 in.	Rolled Edge	13.72
		PLATES (Soup)	
7¾ in.	6 in.	Rolled Edge, Coupe	9.14
9 in.	7 in.	Rolled Edge, Deep Rim	12.96
7 in.	5 in.	Rolled Edge, Deep Rim	8.08
		PLATES (Grill)	
9½ in.		Rolled Edge, 3 Comp. Kress	21.56
9½ in.		Rolled Edge, 3 Comp. Shamrock	25.80
10½ in.		Rolled Edge, 3 Comp. Elite	32.50
13½ in.	Lg.	Chuck Wagon, 3 Comp.	43.10
10½ in.	Sm.	Chuck Wagon, 3 Comp.	32.50
		PLATES (Chop)	
10½ in.	9 in.	Rolled Edge	19.44
11½ in.	10 in.	Rolled Edge	23.68
13½ in.		Chuck Wagon, Plain	38.86
		PLATTERS OR DISHES	
7⅛ in.	4 in.	Rolled Edge	9.14
8¼ in.	5 in.	Rolled Edge	10.42
9¼ in.	6 in.	Rolled Edge	12.74
10½ in.	7 in.	Rolled Edge	14.36
11½ in.	8 in.	Rolled Edge	17.74
12½ in.	9 in.	Rolled Edge	20.82
13⅝ in.	10 in.	Rolled Edge	28.26
15¾ in.	12 in.	Rolled Edge	38.86
19 in.		Special Turkey Platter	130.00
		PITCHERS	
2½ pts.	24s	Hall Boy Jugs	33.48
60 oz.	24s	Rolled Edge, Cable Jugs	52.96
40 oz.	30s	Rolled Edge, Cable Jugs	39.36
21 oz.	36s	Rolled Edge, Cable Jugs	26.14
16 oz.	42s	Rolled Edge, Cable Jugs	19.48
7 oz.	48s	Rolled Edge, Cable Jugs	11.90
4 pts.		Cascade or Ball Ice Jugs	42.68
8 pts.	6s	Rolled Edge, Cable Jugs	105.76

Actual Size	Trade Size	Article	Selling Price
		TEA POTS	
8 oz.		Chicago Teas, Covered	$ 19.44
8 oz.		Boston Teas, Covered	19.66
8 oz.		Tea Pot Lids	6.60
24 oz.		Boston Teas	30.04
32 oz.		Boston Teas	32.86
12 oz.		Hot Water Pot	21.56
		SUGARS	
12 oz.	36s	Covered, Rolled Edge	22.84
17 oz.	30s	Covered, Rolled Edge	26.86
12 oz.		Duquesne, Covered	23.25
17 oz.		Bodies	17.91
		SAUCE BOATS	
3 oz.			16.14
5½ oz.			18.04
9½ oz.			30.38
13 oz.			32.50
		SALADS	
5¾ in.	10 oz.	Footed Salad Bowls	15.08
6½ in.	16 oz.	Footed Salad Bowls	17.32
7½ in.	24 oz.	Footed Salad Bowls	21.66
7 in.	5s	Rolled Edge, Footed	17.42
9 in.	3s	Rolled Edge, Footed	37.01
11 in.	6s	Rolled Edge, Footed	52.28
13 in.		Chuck Wagon Style	104.56
		SPECIALTIES	
½ gallon		Bain Marie Jars	
		Salt & Pepper Shakers	13.08
		ASH TRAYS	
			8.08
		ICE TUBS	
9½ in		Hooped	80.30

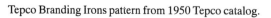

Tepco Branding Irons pattern from 1950 Tepco catalog.

Chapter Nine: The Best of The Rest

Blair Ceramics, Inc.

Hand-painted china is enjoying a surge of popularity and as prices of Watt, Purinton, and Blue Ridge soar; Blair and other lesser known patterns should become more desirable.

William Blair studied at the Cleveland School of Art and after graduating he studied in Europe. He returned to Ohio and apprenticed in ceramics. In an attempt to persuade potteries to change their conventional ways, he contacted major potteries but was rebuffed. "Stick to your painting, sonny," they said. His view of American dinnerware was that it needed a "general over-hauling." "It's downright immoral," Blair was quoted in 1949.

"You see, most American dinnerware today is made by machine on an assembly line, in about the same patterns that have been used for a generation or more. To change their recipe a bit, the manufacturers buy up a few floral designs and paste them willy-nilly on the same old pitchers and plates."

He went on to say, "Then these designs are stamped on over the finished pieces, instead of being baked permanently into the clay base, and after a few months of use, they wear off. All you've got left is a stack of clay slabs. Might as well eat off of a pie tin."

Row 1: Blair Ceramics Plaid bowl, yellow and gray Plaid plate, Plaid jug with spigot, Pryor Plaid mug (not Blair), Plaid covered sugar. Row 2: Pear dessert plate, Plaid salt and pepper, Brick plate, Brick mug, Bird 6" plate, Plaid cup and saucer.

With Blair's innovative new ideas for the time, it's easy to see why he wanted to start out on his own. He and his nephew, Bart Higgins, began to work together toward that goal while still in Ohio. After working all day, William Blair perfected his designs and Bart Higgins blueprinted the molds for what would eventually become Blair Ceramics, Inc. By 1946, they had enough money to head for the Ozarks. After visiting relatives in Ozarks country, he chose a site in Ozark, Missouri. He spent more than a year converting an existing building into the pottery, installing a $15,000 kiln that was shipped from West Virginia. Actual production began in 1946 and soon Blair Ceramics, Inc., employed twenty-five to thirty employees.

All of Blair's casual dinnerware was well made earthenware with semi-vitreous glaze. Early on, there were four hand-painted patterns with Gay Plaid being the most outstanding. The stripes that make up the design on the Gay Plaid pattern are dark green, chartreuse, and cinnamon brown on an ivory background. Gay Plaid was so popular that it was difficult to keep up with demand. It was shipped to the then-48 states and several other points in Canada, Cuba and Hawaii.

William Blair experimented with a line made entirely of red clay. One of the patterns produced was a primitive drawing of a bird on a textured white background bordered in green. The items made in the red clay were very brittle and chipped easily. Blair also did a small line of red clay ware that has the appearance of bricks. Family members tell me they called this pattern Brick.

Production increased steadily but demand was more than could be met by the small plant. In 1953, it was estimated that four times as much product could have been sold had the plant been large enough to handle the production. The pottery was short-lived and went out of business in the 1950s. The molds were sold to an employee of Blair.

Blair hand painted backstamp.

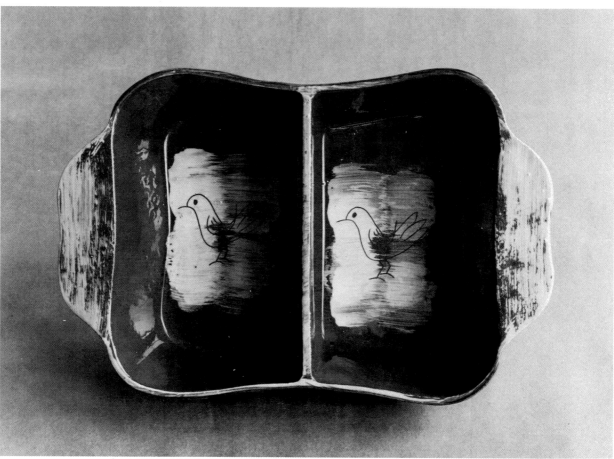

Blair Bird divided vegetable bowl.

Variety of Blair Bird pieces.

Unusual Blair "Dutch Tulip" hand painted bowl.

China Specialties, Inc.

About 1985, Virginia Lee and her son, Joel Wilson, began to work with the East Liverpool, Ohio, potteries specifically for the purpose of bringing out a commemorative mug set for the 50th anniversary of Homer Laughlin's Fiesta dinnerware. Each mug was made in an original Fiesta color. Fewer than 600 mug sets were produced and sales were considered extremely successful. Since the mugs were introduced, the price of the set has risen more than 50 percent.

The unique philosophy of China Specialties, Inc., was to bring to the public a selection of "high style classics, time tested designs that are American designed, American made." The Fiesta dinnerware re-issues met these requirements and the Wilsons began to carry and distribute the new Fiesta.

Hall China in East Liverpool was the next logical move for China Specialties and the now famous Autumn Leaf pattern was a very wise choice of patterns. China Specialties' first Hall China item issued was the Autumn Leaf Airflow teapot with fewer than 2,000 produced.

China Specialties and Hall China have issued several different items in Autumn Leaf, Red Poppy, Silhouette and Crocus. These items are always issued in limited editions and always in items that were never made at the time the wares were originally produced. In no way can these high quality limited editions be construed as reproductions.

Exclusive rights to Hall China patterns have been granted to China Specialties on Hall patterns other than the Autumn Leaf pattern. The Autumn Leaf pattern is a co-exclusive with China Specialties and the National Autumn Leaf Collectors Club. The National Autumn Leaf Collectors Club also has Autumn Leaf pieces made by Hall for their club members.

China Specialties has provided collectors the means of acquiring a collection with the assurance that the production run will not exceed the number announced. It has been proven that all of the Hall limited edition pieces have increased in value. The Autumn Leaf automobile teapot is one of the most desirable China Specialties' limited edition pieces and has increased rapidly in value.

Joel Wilson of China Specialties has provided us with a list of pieces and their date of introduction. If you would like more information, contact China Specialties, Inc., 19238 Dorchester Circle, Strongsville, Ohio 44136.

Pictures and information provided by China Specialties.

1990	Autumn Leaf, Airflow.
1991	Autumn Leaf, set of four, Conic mug, special large handle.
	Autumn Leaf, Norris water server.
	Autumn Leaf, set of four Irish mugs.
	Autumn Leaf, condiment set.
	Autumn Leaf, set of four, onion soup.
1992	Autumn Leaf, super limited, bud vase.
	Autumn Leaf, china memo board.
	Autumn Leaf, playing cards, poker.
	Autumn Leaf, playing cards, double deck pinochle.
	Autumn Leaf, set of four, Libbey wine.
	Autumn Leaf, set of four, Libbey water.
	Autumn Leaf, Hall, set of four, sherbet.
	Auto teapot, plain white.
	Auto teapot, white and platinum.
	Football, teapot, plain sandust.
	Football, teapot, gold/sandust.

Variety of pieces distributed by China Specialties, Inc.

Autumn Leaf, super limited, ashtray.
Auto teapot, plain, green lustre.
Auto teapot, green lustre and platinum.
Football teapot, cobalt blue, plain.
Football teapot, blue and gold.

1993 Autumn Leaf, automobile teapot.
Autumn Leaf, kitchen prayer plaque.
Libbey glass cruet.
Red Poppy, juice reamer.
Auto teapot, yellow and platinum.
Auto teapot, yellow and gold.
Football teapot, plain yellow.
Red Poppy, bud vase.
Silhouette, Airflow teapot.
Silhouette, bud vase.
Autumn Leaf, beer pitcher.
Autumn Leaf, set of four, Pilsner glasses.
Autumn Leaf, juice reamer.
Autumn Leaf, set of four, juice tumbler.
Red Poppy, mustard.
Red Poppy, Airflow teapot.
Silhouette, beer pitcher.
Silhouette, set of four, Pilsner glasses.
Autumn Leaf, baby bean pot.
Autumn Leaf, oval relish.
Ohio Autumn Leaf Show, shot glass.
Autumn Leaf, regular shot glass.
Crocus, auto teapot.

1994 Autumn Leaf, fluted salt and pepper.
Autumn Leaf, pair, hurricane lamp.
Autumn Leaf, set of four, plates (Libbey).
Crocus, mustard.
Red Poppy, set of four, juice glasses.
Red Poppy, set of four, water glasses.
Red Poppy, baby bean pot.
Autumn Leaf, round dome, butter.
Silhouette, cruet.
Crocus, bud vase.
Autumn Leaf, teapot, hook cover.
Autumn Leaf, Fort Pitt, set of four.

Variety of pieces distributed by
China Specialties, Inc.

Coors

In 1873, the Adolph Coors Company was founded. In 1988, in an attempt to lower manufacturing costs at his brewery, Adolph Coors opened a glass factory in Golden, Colorado, for the purpose of producing his own glass beer bottles. Unfortunately, his project did not succeed and the factory closed after only two years. The factory remained closed for fifteen years until the pottery of John J. Herold caught his eye. He became so enchanted with Herold's work that he offered part of his abandoned glass factory to Herold for use as a pottery company. Thus was the Herold China and Pottery Company formed in 1910. Sometime between 1920 and 1921, the name of the company was changed to Coors Porcelain Company.

Although their primary product has been porcelains for chemical and industrial purposes, over the years the company has produced cooking ware, artware and dinnerware. The dinnerware lines were Mello-Tone, Coorado, Golden White, Rockmount and their most successful line--Rosebud 'Cook-N-Serve'.

Rosebud was introduced around 1934. The company produced cooking, serving, dining and baking ware in the Rosebud pattern. Made of low-fire porcelain clay and decorated with the familiar hand-painted rosebud and leaf pattern, Rosebud was originally glazed in four colors: green, rose, yellow and blue with ivory and orange being added later. Mixing bowls were glazed in green, rose, yellow, ivory and blue. Ivory pieces are rare. You can consider yourself lucky if you locate pieces glazed in this color. Orange and yellow are also relatively difficult to find.

With the entrance of the United States into World War II, Coors ceased production of its dinnerware lines to aid in the war effort sometime between 1941 and 1942.

Coors Rosebud casserole. *Photograph by Lonnie Bolding.*

Coors Rosebud batter bowl, salt and pepper.

Crooksville China Company

The Crooksville Art Pottery Company was formed in 1902 in Crooksville, Ohio for the purpose of making vases, pots and other novelty items. The corporation petitioners were Guy E. Crooks, A.P. Tague, W.J. Tague, S.H. Brown and W.H. Brown. They held their first stockholders meeting on January 20, 1902, with J.L. Bennett presiding as president and Guy Crooks as general manager. It was at this first meeting that they changed the name from Crooksville Art Pottery Company to the Crooksville China Company. The first ware made at the new Crooksville China Company was shipped from Crooksville by the Pennsylvania Railroad in February 1903.

The Crooksville China Company gradually increased their production of dinnerware. In 1902, one hundred and twenty-five positions were quickly filled as soon as parts of the new plant became operational.

The Crooksville China Company is credited with creating the first square shape in dinnerware in 1919. The new shape was called Columbia and was a popular shape for many years.

In 1927, an announcement was made regarding installation of a continuous or tunnel kiln to the Crooksville China Company. This expansion was due to steady, continued growth of the company. The announcement was made in conjunction with the company's 25th anniversary.

The Crooksville Pantry BAK-IN line was introduced in 1931. This line filled a need for kitchen ware for the more modern appliances, especially refrigerators. Crooksville's kitchen ware line also matched some of their dinnerware lines. In 1932, new pieces were added to the BAK-IN line. The company was one of the first to market pieces as sets. They produced a covered baker set consisting of underplate and covered baking dish; waffle sets, consisting of large batter jug, syrup jug and utility tray and a fruit juice set. In that year, the Pantry BAK-IN line included five sizes of mixing bowls, two sizes of teapots, two sizes in covered jugs, three sizes in covered baking dishes, cookie jars, a set of four cereal jars and three sizes of covered baking sets.

In 1932, The Crooksville China Company had the capability to produce 600,000 dozens of ware, annually employ 300 people and handle a $315,000 annual payroll.

According to collectors, the best of Crooksville China Company is the Petit Point House pattern, also simply referred to as House, and the Silhouette pattern, consisting of the black silhouettes of two men and a dog. The background is a creamy yellow glaze called Ivo-Glo Glaze.

The Crooksville China Company was forced to suspend operations in 1959. In 1969, part of the Crooksville plant was razed, putting to rest the hopes of another company taking up operation in the plant.

Crooksville China Company circa 1905.

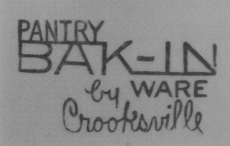

Crooksville China Co. Bak-In backstamp.

Crooksville China Co. Silhouette design decal.

Crooksville China Co. Iva-lure backstamp.

Row 1: Crooksville Petit Point House salt and pepper, individual baker,
Bak-In covered jar, Bak-In small plate, Bak-In bowl. Row 2: Bak-In bowl
set.

Row 1: Crooksville (All Petit Point House decal) Bak-In pie baker, "Fruits"
shape covered bowl, "Fruits" shape platter. Row 2: "Fruits" shape dinner
plate, dessert plate, sugar, cup and saucer, breakfast plate, creamer, sauce
dish, vegetable bowl.

Row 1: Crooksville (All Petit Point House decal) on Radisson shape creamer, pie baker, pie server. Row 2: Oval vegetable bowl, platter.

Row 1: Crooksville (All Petit Point House decal) covered bean pot, teapot. Row 2: Syrup pitcher, batter jug.

Crooksville Petit Point House decal large salver (could be liner for batter set). *All Crooksville Petit Point House from the Collection of Everett Allen.*

Fioriware

Fioriware is a delightful dinnerware line currently being made in historic Zanesville, Ohio. Maddy Fraioli and her husband, Howard Peller, founded Fioriware in 1987. Maddy Fraioli had been a studio potter for seven years before opening the Fioriware Zanesville plant.

Wonderful colors, stylized flowers and leaves make Fioriware a very interesting potential as a future collectible. Fioriware is not inexpensive. However, it is interesting enough to buy for use or to put away as a possible collectible a few years from now. Fioriware also comes in solid colors.

Back row (left to right): Fioriware Harlequin embossed dinnerware, White with Butterscotch, White with Victorian Green, White with Shell Pink, White with Periwinkle. Front row (left to right): Shell Pink Camellia mixing bowl set, Periwinkle Camellia pitcher and large trumpet vase. *Photograph courtesy of Fioriware Co.*

Pictured left to right: Fioriware Vintage mixing bowl set with Garland solid colors and Butterscotch Grape pitcher; Spiral mixing bowl set with Begonia solid colors.

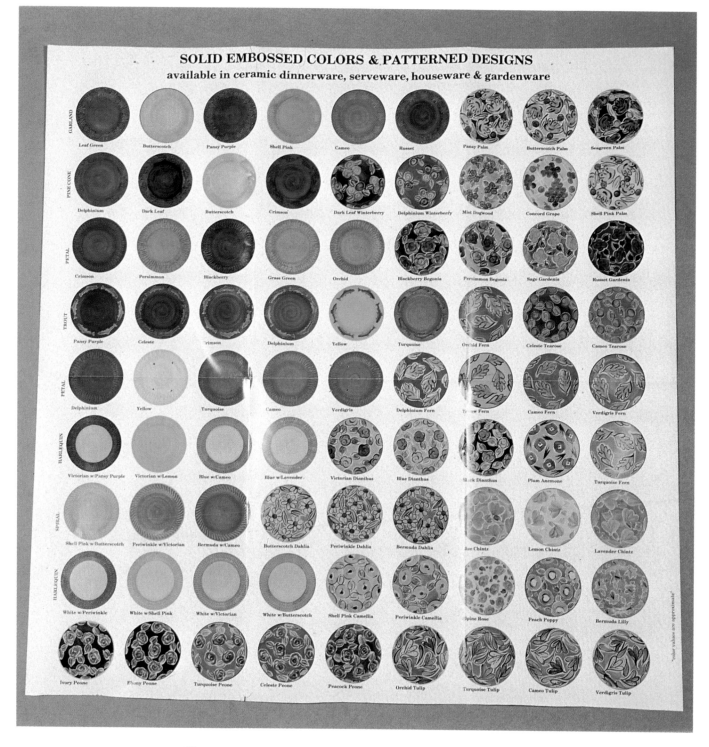

Photograph of Fioriware brochure. *Brochure courtesy of Fioriware Co.*

Frankoma

Frankoma's Wagon Wheel and Mayan-Aztec patterns are the best of Frankoma's dinnerware lines. Both patterns were made in Desert Gold and Prairie Green. For comprehensive information, a "must read" book is *Frankoma and Other Oklahoma Potteries*, by Tom and Phyllis Bess and published by The Schiffer Publishing Company.

John Frank went to Oklahoma in 1927 from Chicago to take a teaching position at the University of Oklahoma in Norman.

In 1933, Mr. Frank opened a small studio pottery in Norman, Oklahoma. Local clays, crude tools and a butter churn for clay making were all of the ingredients necessary for the realization of his vision. He resigned his teaching position in 1936. He and his wife, Grace Lee, began living their dream of providing "beautiful pottery for everyday living."

The first clay they used came from Ada, Oklahoma. "Ada Clay," as it is referred to by collectors, is a creamy beige color. In 1938, the Franks moved to Sapulpa, Oklahoma, where the Frankoma plant is still located. After 1954, red-burning clay became the foundation for their Frankoma ware.

The Frank's daughter, Joniece, literally grew up in the pottery business and managed the Frankoma company for a time after her father's death.

John Frank shown at potter's wheel. Reprinted courtesy of *Sapulpa Herald*.

Row 1: Frankoma Wagon Wheel covered bowl, individual teapot, creamer, teapot, open sugar. Row 2: Cup and saucer, small bowl, vegetable bowl, plate, serving bowl, salt and pepper, candlestick.

Row 1: Fraunfelter covered casserole decorated by Royal Rochester Studios, Apple shape teapot. Row 2: Coffee set (sugar missing) in Farberware frames.

Fraunfelter China Company

The Fraunfelter China Company has a complex history as do many American pottery companies. The Fraunfelter Company was a successor to the Ohio Pottery Company. The Ohio Pottery Company was founded in Zanesville, Ohio, by Jacob Burgy, Charles Applegate and Shepard Humston. The company was incorporated in 1900 for the purpose of producing "specialty stoneware."

In 1904, the Ohio China Company perfected a line of French cooking ware but by 1915 the company was in financial difficulty. It was then that the plant was sold to C.D. Fraunfelter, Dr. H.R. Geyer, Ira B. Mackey, Hugh Hamilton, and H.A. Ernest. C.D. Fraunfelter had previous pottery experience as he had worked at the Roseville Pottery Company for fifteen years. When the plant was taken over by the new owners in 1915, Ohio China Company was producing utilitarian kitchen ware. The new own-

ers brought in John Herold. Herold had been born in Carlsbad, Austria, and trained there as a glass and china decorator. Before going to work for the Ohio China Company, Herold had worked for Weller, J.B. Owens and Roseville Potteries.

During World War I, the Ohio China Company produced items necessary to the war effort such as crucibles, beakers and evaporating dishes. Also during this period, they supplied blanks for women to decorate which was very popular at the time. Ohio China was able to fill the demand created when the European supply ceased to be available. Blanks were also sold to large commercial studios who provided their own decorations.

In 1918, Ohio China Company began producing restaurant ware and in 1922, they introduced Petrascan, a hard porcelain ware.

George E. Fraunfelter displaying plate made for Admiral Byrd's expedition.

The Fraunfelter China Company was formed in 1923 with C.D. Fraunfelter as president, Dr. G.H. Geyer, treasurer, and George E. Fraunfelter as secretary. The new organization absorbed the Ohio China Company of Zanesville and the American China Products of Chesterton, Indiana. Both plants produced hard-glazed china.

During the busy times after the war, Fraunfelter employed 250 people and had showrooms in New York and Chicago. They received many large orders during this period, including the china for the Mayflower Hotel in Washington, D.C. and orders for 41,600 dozen coffee cups for the Childs' restaurant chain.

Fraunfelter China Company went into bankruptcy in 1931 and was purchased by Richard Taylor and was operated by George Fraunfelter. It was at this time that the company provided the china for Admiral Richard Byrd's expedition free of charge. The plates have pictures in blue of the two ships, City of New York and Bear of Oakland and included Admiral Byrd's plane and a sled dog. One plate from the set was kept by George E. Fraunfelter.

Fraunfelter operated until 1939 when it was closed. The company made a quality ware, worthy of notice by the dinnerware collector.

The Hall China Company

The Hall China Company was founded on August 14, 1903, in East Liverpool, Ohio, by Robert Hall. Thirty-three potters were employed. The very first chinaware to bear the name Hall was bedpans and combinets. The tiny company struggled for survival. Whatever plans Mr. Hall had for its future were never known, as he died in 1904.

Upon Mr. Hall's death, his son, Robert Taggart Hall, became the manager. He experimented tirelessly to develop a glaze that would withstand the heat required for "bisque firing." This single-fire process had been used during the Ming dynasty (1368-1644) but all Mr. Hall had to go on was that it had been done before. Robert Taggart Hall developed the first leadless glaze in 1911. The pieces that came out of the kiln were strong, nonporous and crazeproof. Temperatures used in the firing were 2400 degrees Fahrenheit.

World War I gave the Hall China Company an opportunity to furnish ware to the institutional trade. They were able to maintain the world's largest manufacturer of decorated teapots and launched a campaign to educate the American housewife as to the proper methods of brewing tea, and of course, the proper pot was a Hall.

Continued success and obsolete equipment prompted the management to build a new factory in the east end of East Liverpool, Ohio. The plant was completed in 1930 and is still in operation at that site.

Hall China's production is primarily restaurant ware; however, they do make limited editions for China Specialties and the National Autumn Leaf Collectors Club.

Hall China Rainbow Ware bowls.

Rare Crocus teapot made by Hall China Co. *Photography by Phyllis Bess.*

Hall China Crocus 5-1/2" rare Tom and Jerry mugs.

Hall China Crocus cookie jar.

Hall China Crocus electric coffee maker with glass top.

Row 1: Hall China Crocus salt and pepper, sugar and creamer, pitcher,
cup and saucer. Row 2: Bowl set (four sizes), custard baker, plate, salad
bowl.

Row 1: Hall China Crocus mug, utility pitcher, ice lip pitcher, coffee server,
St. Denis cup and saucer. Row 2: Gravy boat, salt, pepper, flour and sugar
shakers and French baker/souffle dish.

Row 1: Hall China Silhouette utility pitcher, pitcher, salt and pepper, plate.
Row 2: Sugar, teapot, creamer, cup and saucer.

Row 1: Hall China Silhouette range set, covered jar, coffee server. Row
2: St. Denis cup, tankard mug, refrigerator set.

Hall China Silhouette waffle iron (Silhouette insert not believed to be made by Hall).

Variety of Cameo Rose pieces made by Hall China for Jewel Tea Co.
Photograph courtesy of Paul Preo.

The Harker Pottery Company

Benjamin Harker, newly arrived from England, bought a farm in East Liverpool, Ohio, on the Ohio River. The farm was rich in clay deposits and Benjamin sold clays to James Bennett. By 1840, Benjamin Harker and his sons, Benjamin Jr. and George, began making and selling yellow-ware by river and wagon.

Benjamin Harker passed away soon after starting the yellow-ware business. During the Civil War, one Harker brother was drafted and the other passed away. David Boyce, a brother-in-law, took over the operation and although the remaining Harker son returned, Boyce was to remain an important name to the Harker operation.

Robert E. Boyce, eldest son of Charles Boyce, became Harker's ceramic engineer in 1927. David Boyce started in sales in 1923 and later became president of the Harker Pottery Company.

Many of the Harker patterns are sought after by collectors. One of the most collectible Harker patterns is the Cameoware line followed by Harker's Red Apple.

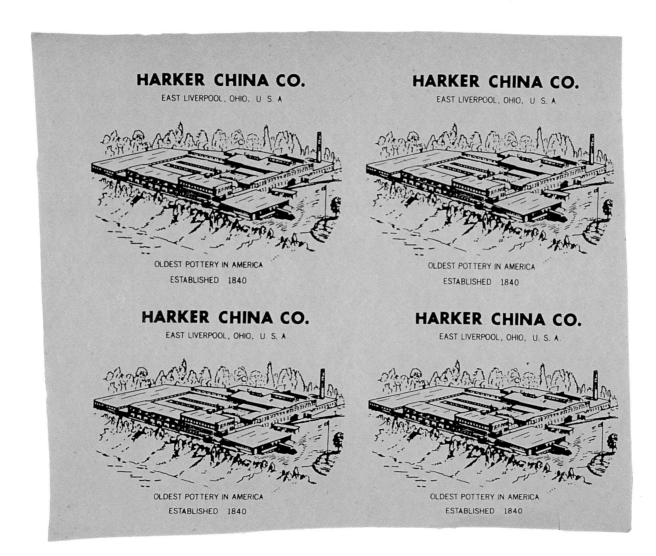

Harker China Co. actual decals.

Actual decals used on Harker China dishes.

Harker China Red Apple hot tile and pie server.

Harker Cameo Shell Ware from *Crockery & Glass Journal*, October 1947.

Harker Cameo Shell Ware from *Crockery & Glass Journal*, October 1947.

Harker White Rose pattern Carv-Kraft made for Montgomery Ward 1942.

Harker White Rose Carv-Kraft backstamp.

The Homer Laughlin China Company

In 1871, the Homer Laughlin China Company began with a two-kiln pottery operated by two brothers, Homer and Shakespeare Laughlin. The brothers operated the pottery together until 1879 when Homer assumed operation of the pottery alone. He produced some of the first whiteware in the country and Laughlin ware received awards as early as 1876.

William Edwin Wells joined Homer Laughlin in 1889. The business was incorporated at the end of 1896. Shortly after, Homer Laughlin sold the business to a Pittsburg group headed by Marcus Aaron and William Wells. Mr. Aaron assumed the presidency of the company and Mr. Wells became secretary-treasurer and general manager. The company relocated to two new and larger plants in Laughlin Station, Ohio, and purchased a nearby working plant for use as their third location. These three plants soon proved to be inadequate and by 1913, the company had two more plants in operation. In 1923, the sixth working plant was built, equipped with continuous tunnel kilns rather than the old periodic kilns. In the years 1927 and 1929, two more plants were added and the old East Liverpool factories were closed down.

William Wells retired from the business in 1930 and was succeeded by his son, Joseph Mahan Wells. Marcus Aaron became chairman of the board and his son, M.L. Aaron, succeeded him as president. Not only did the younger Aaron and Wells continue to manufacture the company's most successful wares, they developed several new lines that transformed domestic dinnerware.

The first of these developments was the Wells Art Glaze line in Matt Green, Peach, Rust, and Melon Yellow. Vellum, with its smooth texture and deep ivory glaze, was used in undecorated ware and served as a base for decorative treatments. Ovenserve and Kitchen Kraft, cooking ware for table use, were developed next. Homer Laughlin proceeded next to the creation of their most popular colored glaze lines--Fiesta, Harlequin and Rhythm. The Eggshell line followed next with its distinctively light and thin china. The company began production of fine translucent table china in 1959 as well as a vitreous line for hotels and institutions.

1956 and 1965 Homer Laughlin Fiesta brochures.

Postcard of Homer Laughlin China Co.

Postcard of loading of kiln at Homer Laughlin China Co.

Row 1: Homer Laughlin Virginia Rose shape covered vegetable bowl, covered butter dish, pitcher, cup and saucer. Row 2: Three sizes of platters, mixing bowl set, salt and pepper, sauce dish, soup bowl, plate.

Homer Laughlin Rose Chinaware decorated by Cunningham & Pickett.

Row 1: Homer Laughlin Suntone (designed by Don Schreckengost) covered sugar, coffee server. Row 2: Teapot, miniature cup and saucer, cup and saucer.

Advertisement for Homer Laughlin China Co. Harlequin Ironstone set.

Robeson Rochester Corporation

The Robeson Rochester Company was formed in 1922 with the coming together of the Rochester Stamping Works and the Robeson Cutlery Company.

The Robeson Cutlery Company was founded in 1893 in Elmira, New York, for the purpose of making cutlery. Robeson's "Shur Edge" cutlery was in such demand that a plant was built in Perry, New York, 40 miles south of Rochester.

In 1888, the Rochester Stamping Company Works began with a tea kettle. After the 1922 merger, Robeson Rochester sold products all over the United States and other countries.

The Robeson Rochester Corporation hand decorated such items as coffee pots, casseroles, creamers and sugars, waffle irons and waffle iron sets. Robeson "Shur Edge" cutlery, Royal Rochester appliances and "Royalite Chinaware" were some of the names of Robeson Rochester products, either manufactured or decorated, in Rochester, New York, in the 1930s.

The Royalite Chinaware and Royal Rochester appliances are by far the most interesting for collectors. Shown is part of a 1930s Royal Rochester catalog showing Royalite Chinaware and Royal Rochester appliances. The experienced collector will readily identify the Fraunfelter company as major providers of china to Robeson Rochester.

Royalite casseroles are listed in the 1930s Royal Rochester catalog in the following patterns, available in either nickel or chrome fittings: Brittany, Golden Pheasant, Fawn and Rose, Modernistic, Royal Bouquet, Cobalt and Pearl, Poppy, Green and Rose, and Orange and Pearl.

Royalite pie bakers (called servers) were available in Modernistic, Royal Bouquet, Golden Pheasant, Fawn and Rose, Brittany, Cobalt and Pearl, Poppy, Orange and Pearl, Green and Rose, and Orange. All were available with nickel and chrome frames except Green and Rose, and Orange. These two patterns were available only with nickel frames.

The Royalite Tea Ball Pots were available in Brittany, Royal Bouquet (two shapes), Fawn and Rose, Cobalt and Pearl, Normandy, Poppy, Cobalt and Pearl, Green and Rose, all with nickel. The Modernistic and Golden Pheasant were available in nickel or chrome.

Robeson Rochester Corporation teapot made by Fraunfelter, marked Royalite Chinaware.

Reprinted from Robeson Rochester 1931 catalog.

"Modernistic" Urn Set

No. 6300388-C Nickel
No. 76300358 Chrome

Nickel	Chrome	Description	Height	Ship. wt.
E-630	E-7630	10 Cup Urn	15 in.	13¾ lbs.
2638	2638	Creamer and Sugar	5¼ in.	3 lbs.
2875	72875	6 Demi Tasse Cups	2½ in.	2¼ lbs.
010388	7010358	Tray—described pages 12 and 10		

16

Reprinted from Robeson Rochester 1931 catalog.

"Golden Pheasant" Urn Set

No. 5900330 Nickel
No. 75900438 Chrome

Nickel	Chrome	Description	Height	Ship. wt.
E-590	E-7590	10 Cup Urn. Faucet and feet blue trim	14¼ in.	11 lbs.
2632	2632	Creamer and Sugar	4½ in.	2¼ lbs.
010330	7010438	Tray—described page 10		

20

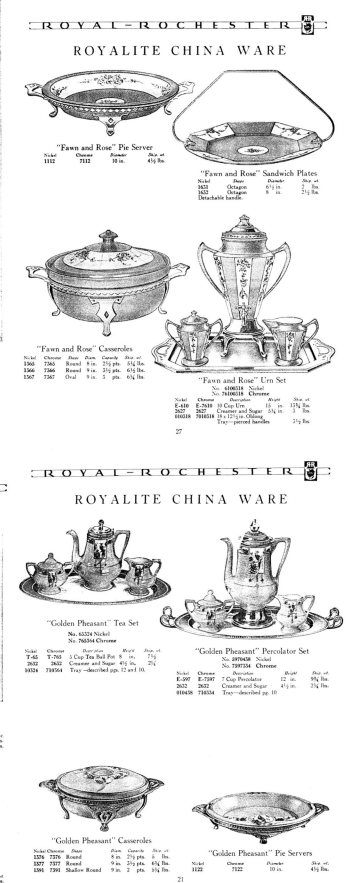

ROYAL-ROCHESTER

ROYALITE CHINA WARE

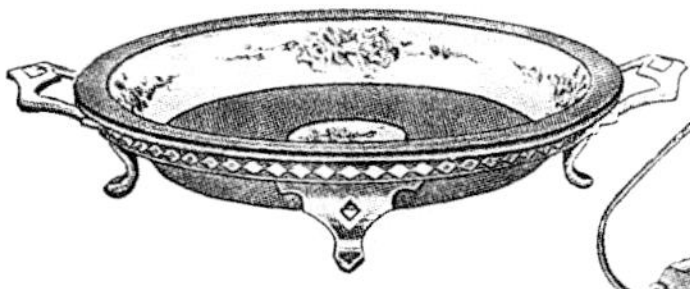

"Fawn and Rose" Pie Server

Nickel	Chrome	Diameter	Ship. wt.
1112	7112	10 in.	4½ lbs.

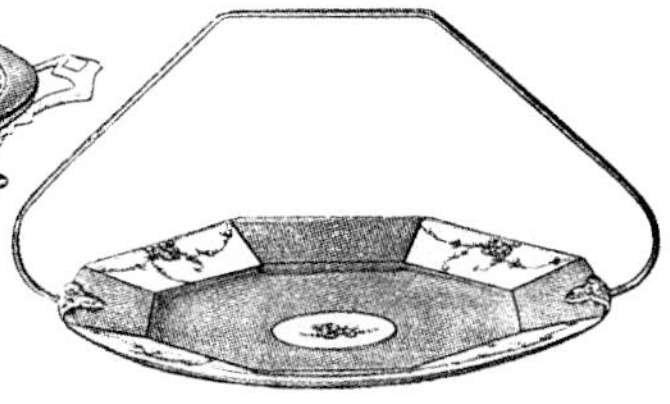

"Fawn and Rose" Sandwich Plates

Nickel	Shape	Diameter	Ship. wt.
1631	Octagon	6½ in.	2 lbs.
1632	Octagon	8 in.	2½ lbs.

Detachable handle.

"Fawn and Rose" Casseroles

Nickel	Chrome	Shape	Diam.	Capacity	Ship. wt.
1365	7365	Round	8 in.	2½ pts.	5¼ lbs.
1366	7366	Round	9 in.	3½ pts.	6½ lbs.
1367	7367	Oval	9 in.	3 pts.	6¼ lbs.

"Fawn and Rose" Urn Set

No. 6100318 Nickel
No. 76100318 Chrome

Nickel	Chrome	Description	Height	Ship. wt.
E-610	E-7610	10 Cup Urn	15 in.	13¾ lbs.
2627	2627	Creamer and Sugar	5¼ in.	3 lbs.
010318	7010318	18 x 12½ in. Oblong Tray—pierced handles		3½ lbs.

27

ROYAL-ROCHESTER

ROYALITE CHINA WARE

"Modernistic" Tea Set

No. 67414-R Nickel
No. 767334 Chrome

Nickel	Chrome	Description	Height	Ship. wt.
T-67	T-767	5 Cup Tea Ball Pot	7 in.	6½ lbs.
2637	2637	Creamer and Sugar	4 in.	2 lbs.
10414-R	710334	Tray—described pgs. 13 and 10		

"Modernistic" Percolator Set

No. 5270374-R Nickel
No. 75270318 Chrome

Nickel	Chrome	Description	Height	Ship. wt.
E-527	E-7527	7 Cup Percolator	11½ in.	9½ lbs.
2638	2638	Creamer and Sugar	5¼ in.	3 lbs.
010374-R	7010318	Tray—described pgs. 13 and 10		

"Modernistic" Casseroles

Nickel	Chrome	Diameter	Capacity	Ship. wt.
1380	7380	8 in.	2½ pts.	5 lbs.
1381	7381	9 in.	3½ pts.	6¼ lbs.

"Modernistic" Pie Server

Nickel	Chrome	Diameter	Ship. wt.
1140	7140	10 in.	4½ lbs.

17

ROYAL-ROCHESTER

ROYALITE CHINA WARE

"Golden Pheasant" Tea Set

No. 65324 Nickel
No. 765364 Chrome

Nickel	Chrome	Description	Height	Ship. wt.
T-65	T-765	5 Cup Tea Ball Pot	8 in.	7½
2632	2632	Creamer and Sugar	4½ in.	2¼
10324	710364	Tray —described pgs. 12 and 10.		

"Golden Pheasant" Percolator Set

No. 5970438 Nickel
No. 7597334 Chrome

Nickel	Chrome	Description	Height	Ship. wt.
E-597	E-7597	7 Cup Percolator	12 in.	9¾ lbs.
2632	2632	Creamer and Sugar	4½ in.	2¼ lbs.
010438	710334	Tray—described pg. 10		

"Golden Pheasant" Casseroles

Nickel	Chrome	Shape	Diam.	Capacity	Ship. wt.
1376	7376	Round	8 in.	2½ pts.	5 lbs.
1377	7377	Round	9 in.	3½ pts.	6¼ lbs.
1391	7391	Shallow Round	9 in.	2 pts.	5¼ lbs.

"Golden Pheasant" Pie Servers

Nickel	Chrome	Diameter	Ship. wt.
1122	7122	10 in.	4½ lbs.

21

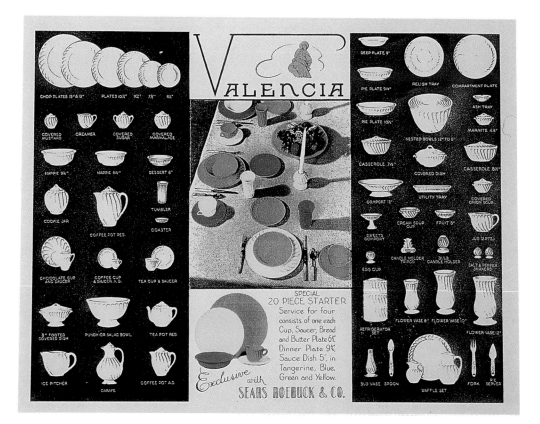

Shawnee advertisement for 20 piece starter set of Valencia dinnerware
sold exclusively by Sears.

Shawnee Pottery Company

The Shawnee Pottery Company was founded in 1937 by
Malcolm Schweiker in Zanesville, Ohio. Mr. Schweiker was
inspecting the site of the American Encaustic Tiling Company
that had closed in 1935 when he "kicked up" a Shawnee Indian
arrowhead. He called his new pottery "Shawnee." The newly
formed Shawnee Company was headed by Addis Hull, Jr., who
served as president, Robert C. Schilling, Vice-President, and
Ernest B. Graham, Secretary.

Americans were in a "Buy American" mode in the late thir-
ties as hostilities toward Germany and Japan were growing.
Retailers were forced to buy American products.

Most of the new pottery's business came from Sears,
Woolworths, Kress, Kresges and other similar stores. Buyers
or representatives of these companies are said to have had a
hand in designing products they ordered from Shawnee Pottery.

Shawnee had its own design staff and included such names

as Rudy Gann who is credited with designing "Smiling Pig,"
"Jack and Jill" and Elephant Cookie jars. Designers also included
Ed Hazel and Louise Bauer, credited with designing Valencia
dinnerware sold through Sears. Bauer is credited with designing the Bauer Valencia advertising piece.

A wartime contract was awarded to Shawnee Pottery in
1942. In 1943, space was rented to the Army with a Major George
Klein in charge. The major's office was the former showroom
of the American Encaustic Tiling Company complete with a
fountain designed by Frederick Rhead.

Shawnee Pottery had a Kenwood Ceramics division.
Kenwood made chafing dishes and casseroles but is best known
for their "Lobster" line of black and white ware with red lob-
sters as handles on the lids. Shawnee's best known line is Corn
Queen and Corn King.

Shawnee Pottery closed its doors in 1961. The pottery had
been under the management of John Bonistall since 1954.

Shawnee Valencia advertising piece designed by Louise Bauer.

Top Row: Green Valencia teapot, Tangerine utility bowl.

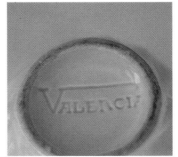

Valencia mark.

Valencia compartment set.

Valencia pitchers: tangerine, green, yellow, burgundy.

Valencia tumblers: green, yellow, blue and tangerine.

Variety of Valencia pieces.

$\mathcal{V}alencia$ •• GAY AS A CARNIVAL •• DURABLE, TOO

$2⁸⁹
20-Pc. Set

A friendly informal meal becomes a festive occasion when your table is set with Valencia ware. Its gay peasant colors captivate your eye. Its *ovenproof* quality saves you labor. Cook and serve in any of these beautiful dishes and bring the food to the table piping hot. Priced lower than comparable colored dinnerware, yet Valencia gives you extra quality in the ovenproof feature. Sets are assorted in Tangerine, Yellow, Blue and Green. Individual pieces in all four colors listed on opposite page. For composition of sets see page 441. *Valencia also shown in color on Page 7.*

20-Pc. Service for 4
Includes 1 complete set in each of the 4 colors illustrated. Shipping weight, 15 lbs.
35 L 4329 . . . . . **$2.89**

32-Pc. Service for 6
2 Blue, 2 Green, 1 Yellow and 1 Tangerine service. Green vegetable dish. 13-in. Blue serving platter. Cereal dishes instead of sauce dishes. Shipping weight, 35 pounds.
35 L 4323 . . . . **$5.49**

35 L 4330—Blue - Yellow - Green - Tangerine. State article and color.

Ice Lip Jug
Holds 64 oz. Shpg. wt., 3 lbs **89c**

Sugar Bowl
Shipping weight, 1 lb. 8 oz **59c**

Cream Pitcher
Shipping weight, 1 lb. 8 oz **39c**

Dinnerware Sold on Easy Payments, See Page 5

Kenwood Lobster dishes.

1941 Sears advertisement featuring Valencia.

Southern Potteries

Blue Ridge is a familiar name to collectors of hand painted dinnerware made by Southern Potteries. Thousands of Blue Ridge pieces were sold for use as premiums at movie theaters. The hand painting allowed the pottery to quickly change a pattern or create a new pattern at no expense.

Collectors tell me that Chintz (shown) is one of the most popular of Southern Potteries' patterns. Any butter dishes, teapots, breakfast sets or unusual pieces are commanding an impressive price. Southern Potteries closed in the 1950s.

Row 1: Southern Potteries Chintz pattern: sugar, tidbit server, coffee or tea server. Row 2: Platter, plate, platter.

Blue Ridge backstamp.

Row 1: Southern Potteries Chintz pattern: handled server, pitcher, candy dish. Row 2: Small platter, dinner plate, luncheon plate, dessert plate.

Taylor, Smith and Taylor

Taylor, Smith and Taylor was founded in 1899 at the Taylor, Smith and Lee facility that had closed about 1896. The Taylor, Smith and Taylor Company was reorganized in 1903. The Taylor interests were bought by W.L. Smith and W.L. Smith, Jr., who held the ownership and management until 1973 when Anchor Hocking purchased the company for their pottery operation.

Taylor, Smith and Taylor is responsible for two lines that are especially favored by collectors. The company's pastel glaze dinnerware line, LuRay Pastels, was introduced in the late 1930s and was produced until the early 1950s.

Solid colored glaze dinnerware lines were very popular in the late 1930s. Taylor, Smith and Taylor's Vistosa is believed to have been introduced in 1938. This solid colored line is not as readily found as LuRay. It is available, however, and readily identified by its "pie-crust" edge. Vistosa can be found in green, mango red, dark blue and yellow.

Row 1: Taylor, Smith & Taylor Vistosa cake plate, footed bowl, sugar, teapot, creamer. Row 2: Cup and saucer, small bowl, breakfast plate, dinner plate, salt and pepper.

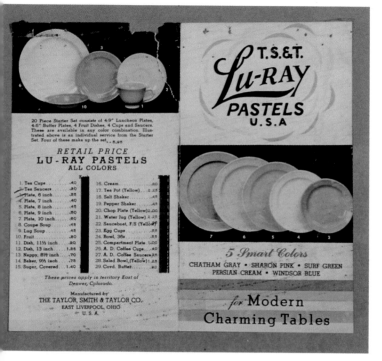

Brochure advertising Taylor, Smith & Taylor Lu-Ray Pastels.

LuRay pastels were introduced in four colors--Windsor Blue, Persian Cream, Sharon Pink and Surf Green. Chatham gray was added at some point in limited quantities. The Chatham gray is difficult to find. The gray was definitely not one of the first four colors but was listed in a 1949 ad.

LuRay pieces listed are from many LuRay ads and information from LuRay collectors.

> Tea cups/saucers.
> Plates, 6", 7", 9", 10".
> Coupe soup-flat.
> Fruit bowl, 5".
> Platters, 11 1/2" and 13".
> Lug soup.
> Bowl, 8 1/2".
> Baker, 9 1/2".
> Sauceboat.
> Pickle dish or liner.
> Covered sugar.
> Covered cream.
> Casserole with cover.
> Tea pot.
> Shaker set.
> Chop plate, 15".
> Water jug, 5 pt.-two other sizes.
> Cake plate (handles).
> Relish dish-divided with center handle.
> Flower vase.
> Bowl, 36s.
> A.D. coffee sets, two styles.
> Cream soup.
> Sauce boat.
> Double egg cup.
> Syrup pitcher.

Lu-Ray Pastels backstamp.

Brochure advertising Taylor, Smith & Taylor Lu-Ray Pastels.

Taylor, Smith & Taylor Lu-Ray Pastels Sharon Pink gravy boat and liner.
Photography by Phyllis Bess.

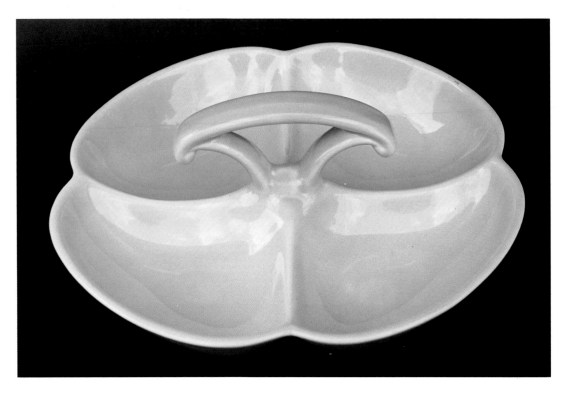

Taylor, Smith & Taylor Surf Green divided relish plate.

Row 1: Taylor, Smith & Taylor Lu-Ray Pastels Windsor Blue A.D. creamer, coffee server, covered sugar. Straight sides, different style of A.D. set. A.D. cups (not shown) also have straight sides, Sharon Pink sugar, Surf Green pot, Windsor Blue creamer. Row 2: Persian Cream plate, Windsor Blue two-handled cream soup, Sharon Pink chop plate, Persian Cream quarter lb. butter dish; Surf Green breakfast plate.

Row 1: Taylor, Smith & Taylor Lu-Ray Pastels, three styles of pitchers, Sharon Pink, Persian Cream and Sharon Pink; Persian Cream teapot. Row 2: Surf Green muffin cover, Windsor Blue egg cup, gray cup/saucer with dark green band, Windsor Blue divided plate, Persian Cream sauce boat, Persian Cream covered casserole.

Taylor, Smith & Taylor Persian Cream flower epergne.

Universal Pottery Company

The Universal Pottery Company was formed in 1934 in Cambridge, Ohio, by a group of Cambridge businessmen. The company is best known to collectors for its Cattail and Ballerina lines.

The Universal Pottery Company sold many lines to grocery stores, movie houses and service stations for use as premium items.

Cattail can be found in a variety of shapes. It can also be found on tinware, glassware and wood items. An oak kitchen table was available from Sears decorated to match the Cattail dinnerware.

Ballerina was also widely distributed and decorated in many different decorations and treatments. The Universal Pottery Company closed its doors in 1960.

Universal Pottery Co. Cattail backstamp.

Universal Pottery Co. Cattail pattern cup and saucer, plate, sugar bowl.

New Tableware Made From Native Perry County Clay

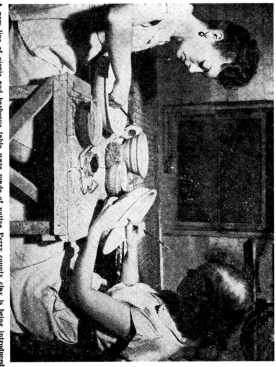

A new line of picnic and barbecue table ware made of native Perry county clay is being introduced by the Watt pottery at Crooksville. For years native clays have not been considered generally to be suitable for table ware since they do not lend themselves readily to the making of delicate and fragile pieces. Mona Young and Betty Riley are shown here doing free-hand underglaze decoration.

Seven days a week, 24 hours a day, the new type ware goes into the kilns in an unending stream.

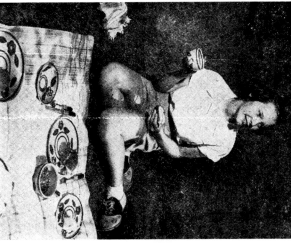

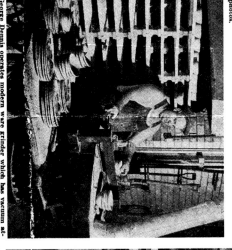

Pretty dishes and pretty girls help make a success of any picnic. Miss Cynthia Schwartz didn't seem to mind drinking lukewarm coffee after posing for Cameraman Chal Milligan, who took these photos.

George Dennis operates modern ware grinder which has vacuum attachment to pick up sharp-edged grindings, helping to prevent silicosis, a major pottery hazard.

Manufacturing technique perfected at Crooksville makes use of native clay mined in the area. All of this ware has an underglaze decoration applied individually by hand, but modern methods make assembly line production possible. Circular table above enables each of three decorators to glaze the same pieces of ware with a different design.

Modern conveyor system carries ware from the decorators. New process was adopted by the Watts firm after 27 years in the manufacture of orthodox stoneware.

Bibliography

BOOKS

Armstrong, Alice Catt (Editor) *Who's Who in California 1961.* Alice Catt Armstrong, 1961.

Derwich, Jenny, and Dr. Mary Latos. *Dictionary Guide to U.S. Pottery and Porcelain.* Jenstan, 1984.

Enge, Delleen. *Franciscan Ware.* Collector Books, 1981.

———, *Franciscan.* Privately published, 1992.

Fridley, A.W. *Catalina Pottery-The Early Years, 1927- 1937.* Rainbow Publishing, 1977.

Gilbert, Dorothy B. (Editor) *Who's Who In American Art.* R.R. Bowker Co., 1962.

Kamm, Minnie Watson. *Old Dishes.* Kamm Publications, 1951.

Kent, Rockwell. *It's Me O'Lord.* Da Capo Press. New York, 1935.

———. *Salamina.* Harcourt, Brace and Company. New York, 1935.

Kerr, Ann. *The Collectors Encyclopedia of Russel Wright Designs.* Schroeder Publishing. Collector Books. Paducah, Kentucky, 1990.

Lehner, Lois. *Lehner's Encyclopedia of U.S. Marks on Pottery, Porcelain and Clay.* Collector Books, 1988.

McKee, Floyd. *A Century of American Dinnerware.* Privately published, 1966.

Moritz, Charles (Editor). *Current Biography 1971.* (32nd Annual Cumulation). The H.W. Wilson Company, 1971.

Nelson, Maxine. *Versatile Vernon Kilns.* Rainbow Publications, 1978.

Overholt, Alma, *The Catalina Story,* Jack Sargent, curator. Catalina Island Museum, edited and updated 1971.

Rehl, Norma. *The Collector's Handbook of Stangl Pottery.* Privately published, 1979.

Schneider, Robert. *Coors Rosebud Pottery,* 1st Edition. Busche-Waugh-Henry Publications, 1984.

Staff. *Who's Who on the Pacific Coast. A Biographical Dictionary of Leading Men and Women of the Pacific Coast States.* Larkin, Roosevelt and Larkin, Ltd. Chicago, 1947.

Stiles, Helen E. *Pottery in the United States.* E.P. Hutton & Co., Inc., 1941.

MAGAZINES AND PERIODICALS

Craig, Edna M. "Background of California Pottery." *China, Glass and Decorative Accessories,* September 1949.

Cunningham, Jo. "California Potteries." *The Glaze,* February 1981.

———. "Westward Ho Dinnerware." *The Glaze,* May 1982.

Kerr, Ann. "Informal." *The Glaze,* May 1981.

———. "Inheritance." *The Glaze,* June 1981.

———. "Intaglio." *The Glaze,* July 1981.

———. "Impromptu." *The Glaze,* April 1981.

———. "Russel Wright's Iroquois Story." *The Glaze,* March 1981.

Sharpe, Patricia. "Brand Name." *Texas Monthly,* December 1991.

Shaw, Paul and Lynn Waits. "Coors Pottery and Porcelain." *The Glaze,* January/February 1982.

Staff. "Ceramics Plant Works Again." *Fortnight,* August 17, 1953. Volume 15, page 23.

Taylor, Frank. "Dining Off the Rainbow." *The Saturday Evening Post,* November 19, 1949.

NEWSPAPERS

Bagby, Sam. "An Old Bottle Launched a Career." *Los Angeles Times,* November 2, 1941.

Field, Zane. "Shawnee, Last Made in 1961, is Suggested." *Collectors Weekly,* December 1, 1970. Volume 2, Number 63.

Schneider, Norris. "Dishes for Byrd Expedition Made by Fraunfelter China Company Here." *The Times Recorder,* January 21, 1962. Section B, page 5.

Staff. "Film Stars Help Dedicate Lavish Ceramics Studio." *The San Francisco Chronicles,* November 20, 1953. Page 17, Column 7-8.

Staff. "Glass, Crystal, Plastic Ware Made in Glendale." *Glendale News Press,* November 26, 1948.

Staff. "Legacy of Ceramist Palin Thorley Will Not Be Lost." *Richmond Times Dispatch,* September 1, 1986.

(Obituary) Goodan, Tillman Parker. *Visalia Times-Delta.* May 26, 1958, Page 9.

(Obituary) Thorpe, Dorothy C., *Los Angeles Times.* September 16, 1989, Part 1, Page 22.

SPECIALTY PUBLICATIONS

Eidbelburg, Martin. *Eva Zeisel: Designer for Industry.* (Catalogue Essay). University of Chicago Press, 1984.

Pickel, Susan. *From Kiln to Kitchen, American Ceramic Design in Tableware.* (Catalog) Illinois State Museum Exhibit, Springfield, Illinois, 1980.

Kent, Rockwell. *Prints, Drawings and Watercolors.* Harbor Gallery, October-November, 1984.

———. *Prints & Drawings 1902-1962.* Associated American Artists, 1987.

Staff. "History of the Hall China Company, East Liverpool, Ohio." *The Bulletin Section.* American Ceramic Society, August 15, 1945, Volume 24, Number 8.

Staff. "Crystal Clear, Dorothy Thorpe's Hobby Turned into a Spectacular Success." (Title of publication unknown). Fidelity Federal Savings & Loan. (Date of publication unknown).

Staff. *Russel Wright, The Original American Modern,* Los Angeles County Museum of Art, Decorative Arts Department.

Thorpe, George A. and Dorothy C. *Dorothy C. Thorpe California.* Privately published catalog, 1941.

Price Guide

Pricing is by far the most difficult task in the book writing process. Prices vary greatly from area to area, shop to shop and dealer to dealer. The collector may expect to pay more for an item at a show than they would at a yard sale.

Prices given in this price guide are just that--a guide. The pricing here is not "the last word" nor is it "gospel." It is a gathering or prices from collectors and dealers around the country and from my personal observations.

Neither the author or the publisher assumes any responsibility for any losses incurred from the use of this guide.

Prices are for mint condition pieces. Pieces that are less than mint should be priced accordingly.

6	T	Left to right, Top row: 30-35 (set); 30-35; 30-35. Bottom row: 95-110; 125-150 (set); 200-225
6	B	Left to right, 150-175; 150-175
8	T	Left to right, 20-25; 15-20; 100-125; 90-100
8	B	Left to right, Top row: 15-20; 30-35; 6-8; 14-16. Bottom row: 20-25; 30-35; 14-16; 25-30
9	T	Left to right, Top row: 300-325; 200-210. Bottom row: 20-25; 15-20; 70-75; 6-8; 10-12 (plate); 18-20 (cov'd. sugar); 8-10 (bowl); 25-30 (ashtray); 10-12 (set)
12	C	Left to right, Top row: 75-80 (w/out lid), 80-100 (w/lid); 75-85. Bottom row: 15-20; 100-120; 20-25; 45-50
13	T	Decorated Country Gardens, Left to right: 500-550 (sm. plate); 550-600
13	B	Country Gardens, Left to right: 250-300 (cov'd. sugar); 400-425 (pitcher); 225-250 (creamer); 325-350 (divided dish)
19	T	Left to right, Top row: 45-50; 20-25; 175-185; 90-100. Bottom row: 150-175 (two-piece set); 18-22; 35-40
19	B	Left to right, Top row: 15-20; 150-175 (set of four); 20-25; 30-35; 40-45; 45-50. Bottom row: 30-35; 30-35 (pair); 35-40; 20-25 (ashtray); 25-30; 30-35; 15-20; 15-20
22	T	Left to right, Top row: 8-10; 15-18; 8-10 (set). Bottom row: 10-12; 15-20; 20-25; 6-8; 4-6
22	B	Left to right, Top row: 8-10 (set); 40-45; 20-25 (pair); 60-65. Bottom row: 30-35; 30-35; 35-40 (set); 20-25 (ashtray); 4-6; 4-6; 4-6
23	T	Left to right, Top row: 20-25; 100-125; 40-45 (two pieces). Bottom row: 20-25 (set); 30-35 (set); 45-50
26	TL	70-75 (Ivy pitcher)
26	B	10-15 (California Ivy Brochure)
28	T	Left to right, Top row: 15-20; 25-30; 6-8; 15-20. Bottom row: 10-15; 12-15 (pair); 15-20; 18-20 (cruet); 18-20 (cruet); 8-10 (set); 15-20
28	B	Left to right, Top row: 100-125; 70-75; 70-75; 20-25; 10-15. Bottom row: 10-15; 18-20; 20-25; 30-35
29	B	Antique Grape, Left to right: 5-10; 8-10; 10-12 (set)
30	T	Left to right, Top row: 8-10 (set); 8-10; 15-20 (set). Bottom row: 4-6; 10-12 (pair); 6-8; 4-6
30	B	Left to right, Top row: 10-15; 15-20 (two pieces); 15-20. Bottom row: 10-15 (set); 10-15 (set)
31	T	Left to right, Top row: 10-15; 25-30; 20-25 (set). Bottom row: 6-8; 10-12 (set); 15-20; 4-6; 15-18 (pair); 20-30 (two pieces)
32	T	Left to right: 15-20 (set); 20-22; 10-15; 5-10
33	T	Left to right: 15-20 (set); 20-25; 15-18; 20-25 (pair); 8-10
33	B	Left to right, Top row: 50-55; 40-45; 60-65. Bottom row: 10-15 (pair); 15-20; 10-12 (set); 20-25 (set)
34	C	70-75
35	T	Left to right: 20-25 (set); 6-8; 20-25
35	B	Left to right, Top row: 20-25; 40-45; 6-8. Bottom row: 20-25; 15-20 (pair); 25-30; 20-25 (set)
36	B	Left to right: 95-100 (cheese pl.); 125-135 (snack pl.); 85-95 (carafe); 55-60 (divided pl.); 40-45 (gravy boat)
37	T	25-35
40	BL	40-45
41	T	Left to right: 15-20 (w/out lid), 20-25 (w/lid); 8-10; 6-8
44	T	Left to right: 60-65; 45-50 (set); 65-75
45	B	Left to right, Top row: 8-10 (set); 30-35 (w/out lid), 35-40 (w/lid); 35-40. Bottom row: 8-10; 15-20; 30-35; 10-15 (pair); 15-20
47		Left to right: carafe 40-45, 45-50, 40-45, 50-55, 15-20 (set), 15-20 (set)
48	T	Left to right: 10-15 ea. (fish plates); 25-30 ea. (Baker, complete w/metal frame)
55	B	80-85 (Wallace pitcher)
56	B	Left to right: 12-15 (set); 18-20; 6-8
60	T	10-15 (shakers, pair); 25-30 (handled relish); 10-12 (dinner plate); 14-16 (cup/saucer, set)
60	B	25-30
61	T	20-25
62	C	Left to right, Top row: 45-50; 25-30; 35-40. Bottom row: 30-35; 25-30; 20-25
63	T	Left to right, Top row: 45-50; 55-60; 45-50; 35-40; 45-50. Bottom row: 20-25; 45-50; 25-30; 50-55; 40-45; 50-55
63	BL	25-30
64	T	Left to right, Top row: 15-20; 30-35. Bottom row: 10-15; 25-30; 15-20; 15-20
65	T	Left to right: 45-50; 55-65; 40-45
65	B	Left to right, Top row: 45-50; 60-65; 35-40; 35-40; 50-55. Bottom row: 60-65; 40-45; 75-80; 35-40; 35-40; 35-40
66	T	Left to right, Top row: 15-20; 25-30; 35-40; 40-45. Bottom row: 45-50; 45-50; 35-40; 35-40; 45-50; 15-20
67	T	Left to right, Top row: 35-40; 35-40; 35-40; 35-40; 35-40. Bottom row: 25-30; 15-20; 30-35; 15-20; 30-35; 15-20; 45-50; 15-20; 30-35
68	T	Left to right, Top row: 55-60 (set); 45-50 (set); 45-50; 15-20; 35-40. Bottom row: 20-25; 30-35; 30-35; 30-35; 15-20
68	B	Left to right, Top row: 45-50; 20-25; 15-20; 25-30; 45-50. Bottom row: 15-20; 15-20; 15-20; 15-20
69	T	Left to right, Top row: 65-75; 70-75; 110-115. Bot-

Collectible Dinnerware
Price Guide Continued

133	T	Left to right, Top row: 45-55; 50-55; 65-70. Bottom row: 45-55; 65-70; 50-65 (set)
133	B	Left to right, Top row: 60-75; 35-40; 60-75; 50-75; 15-18; 35-40. Bottom row: 50-75; 35-40; 40-45
134	T	Left to right, Top row: 50-55 (set); 200-225; 40-45. Bottom row: 35-40; 60-65 (Wallace dinner pl.); 75-85 (indiv. creamer); 100-125 (syrup or creamer)
134	BR	100-125
135	T	Left to right, Top row: 35-45; 30-35; 60-65; 50-55 (set); 30-35. Bottom row: 175-200; 35-40; 65-75
135	B	Top row: 65-75. Bottom row: 45-55; 35-40; 55-65
136	T	Left to right: 175-185; 125-150
136	B	Left to right, Top row: 40-50; 75-85; 100-125; 30-35. Bottom row: 40-45; 60-75; 95-100; 65-75; 25-30; 25-30
137	T	Left to right, Top row: 45-50; 45-50 (creamer/sugar, set); 65-75. Bottom row: 50-60 (cup/saucer, set); 40-50 (salt/pepper, pair); 25-30; 25-30; 75-80
137	B	200-250
138	T	Left to right, Top row: 75-85 (set); 150-175; 60-65. Bottom row: 65-75; 45-50 (straight-sided jar); 35-45; 100-125; 150-175
138	B	Left to right, Top row: 75-85; 95-100; 35-40. Bottom row: 40-45; 35-40; 75-80; 65-75
141	B	Left to right, Top row: 10-12; 6-8; 100-125 (water cooler); 4-6; 15-18. Bottom row: 10-15; 12-15 (pair); 6-8; 12-15; 2-3; 12-14 (cup/saucer, set)
142	B	25-30
143	T	10-15 (cup/saucer, set); 10-12 (dinner plate); 10-12 (salt/pepper, pair); 25-30 (vinegar cruet)
143	B	40-45 (unusual Blair bowl)
144	BL	For current pricing, contact China Specialties (see pg. 144)
145		(All pictured): For current pricing, contact China Specialties (see pg. 144)
146	TR	50-60
146	B	50-55; 20-25 (pair)
148	T	Left to right, Top row: 20-25 (pair); 8-10; 20-25; 6-8; 20-25. Bottom row: 45-50; 40-45; 35-40
148	B	Left to right, Top row: 10-12; 35-40; 20-25. Bottom row: 10-12 (dinner plate); 6-8 (small plate); 10-15 (sugar); 8-10 (breakfast plate); 10-15 (cup/saucer, set); 10-15 (creamer); 4-6 (sauce dish); 15-20 (veg. bowl)
149	TL	Left to right, Top row: 10-15; 15-20; 30-35. Bottom row: 15-20; 15-20
149	TR	Left to right, Top row: 100-125; 70-75. Bottom row: 40-45; 45-55
149	B	25-30
152	B	Left to right, Top row: 35-45; 20-25; 10-15; 25-30; 10-15. Bottom row: 8-12 (cup/saucer, set); 4-6 (sm. bowl); 15-20 (bowl); 15-18 (plate); 25-30 (serving bowl); 10-15 (salt/pepper, pair); 30-35 (candlestick)
153	T	Left to right, Top row: 35-45; 45-50. Bottom row: 20-25; 45-50
155	B	Left to right: 15-20; 20-25
156	T	1250-1500 (rare Crocus teapot)
156	B	125-150 ea. (rare Crocus Tom & Jerry mugs)
157	TL	110-125
157	BR	250-300
158	T	Left to right, Top row: 35-40; 30-35; 25-30; 150-175; 12-15 (set). Bottom row: 75-85 (set of three); 45-50 (sm. mixing bowl); 20-25 (custard); 10-12; 20-25
158	B	Left to right, Top row: 45-50; 45-50; 60-65; 75-85; 50-60. Bottom row: 30-35; 15-20 (salt shaker); 15-20 (pepper shaker); 90-100 (flour shaker); 90-100 (sugar shaker); 20-25
159	T	Left to right, Top row: 35-40; 140-150; 40-45 (pair); 12-15. Bottom row: 20-25; 275-300; 18-20; 12-15 (cup/saucer, set)
159	B	Left to right, Top row: 20-25 (salt); 30-35 (drippings jar); 20-25 (pepper); 135-145; 110-120; 50-55 (St. Denis cup/saucer, set). Bottom row: 45-50; 75-85 (sq. cov'd. refrig. dish); 50-60 (rect. cov'd. refrig. dish)
160	T	125-135
160	B	10-12 (sm. plate); 4-6 (sauce dish); 40-50 (butter); 50-60 (teapot); 14-18 (salt/pepper, pair); 10-12 (dinner plate); 10-12 (cup/saucer, set)
161	B	15-20 per sheet (Harker China Co. decals)
162	T	15-20 (car decals); 20-25 (cherry decal); 30-35 (barn decals)
162	B	25-30; 35-40
166	B	15-20 (1956 Fiesta brochure); 10-15 (1965 Fiesta brochure)
167	T	10-15 (Homer Laughlin postcard)
167	C	10-15 (Homer Laughlin postcard)
167	BR	Left to right, Top row: 35-40; 40-45; 40-45; 8-10 (cup/saucer, set). Bottom row: 15-20 (sm. platter); 20-25 (med. platter); 25-30 (lg. platter); 25-30 (sm. bowl); 30-35 (med. bowl); 35-40 (lg. bowl); 15-20 (salt/pepper, pair); 4-6 (sauce dish); 15-18 (flat soup); 8-10 (plate)
168	T	Set of Homer Laughlin Melody pattern on Rhythm shape (called Rose on p. 168). Decorated by Cunningham & Pickett, Alliance, Ohio 1955. Set includes 6 pl. settings, serving bowl, creamer/sugar set. Entire set in box, 150-175
168	BL	Left to right, Top row: 15-20; 40-45. Bottom row: 35-40; 50-60 (mini cup/saucer, set); 8-10 (cup/saucer, set)
169	T	10-15 (Harlequin brochure)
170	TR	45-50
172	T	10-15 (Valencia brochure)
173	L	250-300 (Valencia advertising piece)
173	R	Top row: 45-50. Bottom row: 20-25
174	TL	150-200
174	B	Left to right: 35-45; 35-45
175	T	Left to right: 15-20 ea. (Pastel tumblers have been reported in slate blue, pink, lt. green, pale green)
175	B	Left to right: 35-45; 35-45
176	T	10-12 (salt/pepper, pair); 10-15 (creamer); 15-20; 6-8 (plate); 10-15 (cup/saucer, set)
177	T	35-40
178	B	Left to right, Top row: 20-25; 95-110 (rare); 150-175. Bottom row: 20-25; 15-20; 20-25
179	B	Left to right, Top row: 90-95; 145-165; 75-85. Bottom row: 30-35; 15-20; 15-18; 4-6
180	B	Left to right, Top row: 20-25; 165-175; 25-30; 40-50; 15-20. Bottom row: 10-15 (cup/saucer, set); 6-8; 10-12; 12-15; 30-40 (salt/pepper, pair)
182	T	35-45
182-83	B	Left to right, Top row: 20-25; 95-110; 25-30; 45-50; 150-175; 40-45. Bottom row: 12-15; 25-30; 30-35; 25-30; 15-18
184	T	Left to right, Top row: 110-120; 45-50; 50-55; 40-45. Bottom row: 85-95; 10-15 (egg cup); 10-15 (cup/saucer, set); 15-20 (divided plate); 25-30 (gravy boat); 65-75 (cov'd. casserole)
184	BL	120-130 (LuRay flower epergne)
185	B	Left to right: 12-14; 10-12; 14-16

tom row: 65-70; 60-65; 60-65

70	T	Left to right: 140-150; 100-110
71	T	150-160
71	B	300-310
72	T	Left to right, Top row: 75-85; 65-75. Bottom row: 50-55; 115-125; 50-55
72	B	Left to right: 115-125; 50-55
73	T	Left to right, Top row: 95-100 (set). Bottom row: 30-35; 25-30
74	T	Top row: 75-80 (set). Bottom row: 75-80 (set)
76	B	Left to right, Top row: 40-45; 40-45; 20-25. Bottom row: 25-30 (set, w/out lid), 30-35 (set, w/lid); 30-35 (set)
77	T	Left to right, Top row: 50-60 (cream/sugar, set); 20-25 (plate); 45-50; 125-150 (serving pitcher). Bottom row: 25-30 (set); 15-20; 30-35 (pair); 25-30; 40-45 (w/liner); 45-50
79	B	250-300
80	B	100-125 (tumbler); 150-160 (large salver)
82	T	60-65
84	B	Left to right: 45-50; 10-15
85	TL	Price not known
91	T	25-30
98	TL	350-425 (complete)
98	C	125-150
98	B	Left to right: 20-25 (bowl); 20-25 (plate); 25-30 (cup and saucer)
99	B	Left to right, Top row: 15-20; 20-25; 30-35. Bottom row: 15-20 (divided veg.); 10-15 (cov'd. sugar); 15-20 (sauceboat/liner); 10-15 (fruit compote); 15-20 (veg. bowl); 10-12 (set); 15-20 (relish tray); 6-8 (br/butter plate); 20-25 (creamer)
100	B	Left to right: 6-8; 10-12; 10-12 (set)
101	T	Left to right, Top row: 20-25 (pair); 25-30; 15-20 (w/out lid), 20-25 (w/lid); 20-25 (w/out lid), 25-30 (w/lid); 40-45. Bottom row: 10-15; 10-15 (set); 8-10 (salad plate); 10-15 (sugar bowl); 10-15 (veg. bowl); 8-10 (sm. bowl); 10-12 (dinner plate)
103	T	Left to right: 45-50; 40-45; 35-40
105	B	Left to right, Top row: 15-20; 20-25; 65-75; 20-25 (set)
106	B	Left to right: 12-15 (bowl); 15-20 (serving plate); 8-10 (sm. bowl); 8-10 (creamer); 6-8 (cup); 6-8 (plate); 15-18 (gravy boat/liner)
108	T	Left to right: 20-25 (pair); 18-20 (creamer); 20-25 (sugar); 20-25 (cup/saucer, set); 18-20 (plate); 550-600 (cov'd. butter)
108	C	275-300

108	B	35-40 (sugar/creamer, set); 25-30 (cup/saucer, set); 550-600 (cov'd. butter)
109	TR	20-25 (plate); 25-30 (cereal bowl); 20-25 (sm. bowl); 25-30 (cup/saucer, set)
109	BL	40-50 (coffee bottle); 25-30 (demi cup/saucer, set)
111	B	6-8 (sm. plate); 10-15 (bowl); 15-20 (veg. bowl); 6-8 (sm. bowl)
112	BL	45-50
113	T	Prices not established for these pieces
115	B	15-20 (sm. bowl); 15-20 (sm. bowl); 25-30 (coaster); 45-50 (creamer/sugar, set); 35-40 (cov'd. soup); 20-25 (gravy boat); 40-45 (salt/pepper, pair)
116	TL	50-60
116	BR	Prices not established for these pieces
120	T	Left to right, Top row: 4-6 (br/butter plate); 25-30 (marmite); 10-12 (creamer); 20-25 (lg. salad). Center row: 15-18 (sugar w/lid); 30-35 (teapot); 10-15 (cup/saucer, set). Bottom row: 6-10 (fruit bowl); 8-10 (dinner plate)
122	TR	Left to right: 10-12 (cup/saucer, set); 35-40 (coffee server); 10-15 (creamer); 15-20 (sugar)
122	B	10-12 (Century shape)
123	T	Left to right: 75-85; 35-40; 45-55
123	B	125-150 (set of three, cov'd. jars)
124	T	350-400
125	T	Hyalyn prices not established
126	B	Left to right, Top row: 15-20; 10-15 (set); 15-20 (set); 30-35; 10-15. Bottom row: 10-12; 10-15; 20-25 (set); 15-20
127	TR	Left to right, Top row: 12-15; 25-30; 8-10. Bottom row: 15-18; 12-15; 10-12 (set); 30-35; 10-12 (salt/pepper, pair); 15-18 (tumbler); 6-8 (bowl); 2-3 (saucer); 8-10 (creamer); 6-8 (bowl); 4-6 (sm. bowl)
127	BL	Left to right, Top row: 15-20; 15-18; 40-45; 30-35. Bottom row: 8-10; 10-15; 8-10
128	TL	15-18
128	TR·	90-95 (as pictured), 100-125 (if complete)
128	B	12-14 ea.
129	T	Left to right: 12-15 (veg. bowl); 8-10 (platter); 6-8 (plate); 14-16 (platter); 8-10 (sugar); 12-15 (creamer); 25-30 (teapot); 10-15 (gravy boat)
129	BL	20-25
130	T	50-60 (Calla Lily plate)
130	BL	75-85 (American Way plate)
131	T	Left to right: 150-200; 125-150
132	BR	Left to right, Top row: 125-150; 50-75; 125-150. Bottom row: 75-100 (set); 50-75

Index